THE ECONOMIC SYSTEM & INCOME DISTRIBUTION IN YUGOSLAVIA

D0169103

THE ECONOMIC SYSTEM & INCOME DISTRIBUTION IN YUGOSLAVIA

HENRYK FLAKIERSKI

M. E. Sharpe, Inc.
ARMONK, NEW YORK
LONDON, ENGLAND

Available in the United Kingdom and Europe from M. E. Sharpe,
Publishers, 3 Henrietta Street, London WC2E 8LU.

Published simultaneously as Vol. 27, No. 4 of
Eastern European Economics

Library of Congress Cataloging-in-Publication Data

Flakierski, Henryk.
    The economic system and income distribution in Yugoslavia /
Henryk Flakierski.
        p.   cm.
    ISBN 0-87332-605-9
    1. Income distribution—Yugoslavia. 2. Management—
Yugoslavia—Employee participation. 3. Yugoslavia—Economic
policy—1945–
I. Title.
    HC407.Z9I51472   1989   89-36369
    338.9497—dc20   CIP

Printed in the United States of America

MA 10 9 8 7 6 5 4 3 2 1

Contents

Henryk Flakierski is professor of economics, York University, Toronto.

Preface

For some time now I have been investigating the relationship(s) between the degree of decentralization of the economic system and inequality of pay. My most recent work—*Economic Reform and Income Distribution: A Case Study of Hungary and Poland* (M. E. Sharpe, 1986)—examines the nature of this relationship in two East European socialist countries. In the present work I intend to examine the relationship between the self-management system of Yugoslavia and the income distribution pattern in that country.

It is unfortunate that so little work has been done on income distribution in the East European socialist countries. Nor have there been detailed investigations of the effect of decentralization of the economic mechanism on income distribution in these countries. It is the aim of this study to make a contribution to this problematic.

Of course, while the Yugoslav case may be illuminating, the relationship between income distribution and the economic system in other East European countries must also be considered if we are to draw any larger conclusions. But a comparative study of these countries would be a daunting task, given the inadequacy of their statistics on income inequality. For many years this area of statistics has been ''ideologically sensitive'' and deliberately neglected. Accordingly, I consider this study to be a part of an ongoing research project that began with my studies of Hungary and Poland and will be expanded in the future to countries not yet analyzed.

The present work consists of five chapters. The first is a brief survey of changes in the Yugoslav economic system since 1945, with special emphasis on changes in distribution principles and policies. The major systemic changes are dealt with only insofar as they help to explain the distribution of income.

In the second chapter I present a statistical analysis of pay inequalities in Yugoslavia for the period 1964-1983, and in chapters three and four, on this basis, I attempt to define the relationship between pay differentials and the socioeconomic characteristics of Yugoslavia's self-management system. The greater length of the fourth chapter, on interbranch differentials, is a reflection not of its relative importance but rather of the fact that there is a huge theoretical literature on this subject which required critical review.

Finally, in the fifth chapter I shall attempt to draw some conclusions from the analysis.

* * *

I should like to thank the members of the economics department of the University of Belgrade for their hospitality and their help in collecting materials during my visits to Yugoslavia in March 1985 and May 1987. I also gained greatly from consultations with colleagues at the Institute of Economics in Zagreb. Special thanks are due to Professor R. Stojanović for arranging my trip to Yugoslavia and numerous meetings with other scholars.

I was also privileged to participate in a seminar on Economic Problems in the Communist Countries, led by professors W. Brus, M. Kaser, and F. Seton. Their comments on my working paper on Yugoslavia helped me a great deal.

Many friends and colleagues have been kind enough to read all or part of this manuscript at various stages of completion and to offer valuable criticisms and suggestions. Among them, special thanks are due to W. Brus for commenting on initial drafts of my work. I owe a debt of gratitude as well to my teaching assistant, George Stubos, for his valuable suggestions and his editorial polishing of my final manuscript. Last, but not least, thanks to the Canada Council. Without their generous financial assistance this project could not have been undertaken.

All of these contributions helped to make this book possible. Needless to say, none of the above-mentioned people or institutions is in any way responsible for the views I have expressed, or for errors my analyses may contain.

Toronto 1989

THE
ECONOMIC
SYSTEM
&
INCOME
DISTRIBUTION
IN YUGOSLAVIA

CHAPTER I

A Survey of Systemic Changes

It is not our intention in this survey to describe the process of change in the Yugoslav economic system in a comprehensive way. The reader will find a very detailed description of its evolution in Branko Horvat's book *The Yugoslav Economic System* (M. E. Sharpe, 1976). Here we will concentrate on systemic changes only to the extent that they help us to understand certain changes in distribution principles and policies in Yugoslavia in the postwar period.

In looking at Yugoslavia's postwar economic system we can distinguish two main periods: a period of centralism lasting from 1945 until 1952; and the period from 1952 to the present, during which the Yugoslav self-management system has evolved. In this second period, from the point of view of systemic changes, we can distinguish: (a) the 1952-1965 period of decentralization, sometimes called the period of "formal" self-management; (b) the reform period of 1965-1972/74; and (c) the time since the reform, called the social planning period, which extends up to the present and is now in the process of major change.

1. The Period of Traditional Centralism, 1945-1952

In the immediate postwar period the earnings distribution system in Yugoslavia was a copy of the Soviet one. The state established fully detailed skill differentials for all jobs, occupations, and trades in different branches and sectors of the economy. Work norms were also set by the state, and overfulfillment of them was rewarded with extra pay. For managerial personnel there were premiums and bonuses for fulfillment and overfulfillment of the state plan.

During this period both skill differentials and interbranch differentials were very small, and the role of rationing was still substantial. Such arrangements were in some respects inevitable, given the economic devastation of the country due to the war, and the urgent need for reconstruction. Thus, the relative equality of incomes may be seen as a product of the material conditions prevailing in Yugoslavia at the time.[1]

Another expression of this egalitarian trend was a sharp decline in the relative position of civil servants and office employees in comparison with the prewar period. It is significant that manual workers achieved near-parity in terms of pay with civil servants, whereas in the prewar period this stratum had received twice the pay of manual workers.[2]

The egalitarian ethos of the partisans also contributed to the elimination of social differences in Yugoslavia—differences that were very substantial before the war. The almost complete elimination of various capitalist forms and the restriction of landholdings to 10 hectares (25 acres) decisively undermined the previous causes of economic inequality.

2. The Post-Centralism Period

"Formal" self-management (1952-1965)

In the early 1950s Yugoslavia abandoned the traditional centralist model. The leadership was determined to decentralize the economy and introduce self-management in the enterprises. The groundwork for the New Economic System (NES) was laid in July 1950, with the enactment of a law giving workers' collectives authority over the management of state enterprises and the various economic associations. Although the NES did not became operational until 1952, the government began reorganizing the central planning apparatus along with its ministries and directorates in 1951. The detailed central planning of production was gradually reduced in favor of strategic planning of basic proportions. The relation between the macro plans and the micro plans was made more flexible. Enterprises were given more autonomy.

Where income distribution is concerned, the egalitarian trend was gradually reversed after 1952. Trade unions and other social organizations demanded that skill differentials be increased and that more discretionary income be left to the enterprise. The intention was to increase the allocation for bonuses and to strengthen the role of work-oriented wages, sometimes reducing the nonwage benefits in the total pay. Workers' councils were empowered to determine the wage differentials and work incentives in the enterprises, under the supervision of the commune and the trade unions.

After 1952 a planned parameter for every industry and branch was established as the basis for determining the proportion of wages and profits in the income of the enterprise. This parameter—called the rate of accumulation and funds—became the foundation for the calculation of a profit-wage ratio, established by the following procedure. The expected income of the enterprise and the corresponding planned wage bill were determined on the basis of the social plan. The difference between gross income (without depreciation) and the planned wage fund was called accumulation and funds (AF); what this represented was the expected gross profit. This magnitude (AF), divided by the planned wage fund (average wage rate in the branch or industry multiplied by the planned number of employees), was labeled the rate of accumulation and funds, which was nothing else but an average branch ratio of expected gross profit to the planned or standardized wage bill. This parameter of distribution was used for the establishment of the actual wage bill in the enterprises of a particular branch by multiplying the actual gross income of these enterprises by the rate of accumulation and funds. The system of AF rates was a compromise between complete, direct administrative control and some form of enterprise autonomy, and it was conducive to labor-saving incentives.

Some shortcomings of the AF system soon led to its demise. The AF rate was not uniform for the whole economy, but was different for different branches and industries, and thus created unequal conditions of economic activity. Furthermore, due to the aggregate nature of the AF parameters and a lack of precision, some enterprises within each branch ended up receiving wages much above the standardized wage bill. The government was forced to introduce a tax on "extra wages" (the difference between the actual wage bill and the standardized one). For their part, enterprises, in order to reduce the taxable "extra wages," tried to reduce their actual wage bill by hiring less-skilled workers or by registering fictitious ones. In response to these unforeseen developments, the state tried to differentiate the tax rate on the basis of skill categories. By 1954, however, it became obvious that the system was unmanageable, and it was replaced by an "accounting wage'' system which survived until 1958.

The new system divided the wage fund into two components: accounting wages and wages out of profit. Accounting wages were derived by applying prescribed wage rates to skill categories multiplied by actual working time. These prescribed wage rates were controlled by an agreement among the enterprise, the trade unions, and the local government.[3] In effect, the accounting wages were wages fixed in advance. Despite considerable trade union and local government control over accounting wages, enterprises were quite successful in increasing them by raising wage rates and reducing work norms. The incentive to do so was strengthened by the fact that profits were taxed at a rate of 50%, creating a strong pressure to reduce profits and increase accounting wages.

The other part of wages was conceived as a variable wage—a reward the worker or manager received from the enterprise at the end of the accounting period as a supplementary wage payment out of current profits.[4] Usually, this supplementary wage was calculated as a certain differentiated percentage of the fixed wages of particular jobs and occupations. It is worth stressing that the structure of variable wages, unlike that of fixed wages, was not regulated by the federal government.

Although between 1952 and 1961 there were legislative changes to the principles establishing the fixed wages, two basic tools were the point of departure for introducing fixed wages into the enterprise; namely, the minimum wage set annually and the average wage rates for nine separate skills and qualifications, both established by the federal government. All enterprises were obliged to produce a wage structure for these categories that conformed to the federal government's guidelines, and the communes were entrusted to oversee the implementation of these guidelines.[5] However, it soon became apparent that these measures to control the skill structure of wages were ineffective. First, the federal minimum wage was lower than the lowest wage actually paid, and second, enterprises were able to disperse pay widely within each skill and occupation, and yet still conform to state guidelines. This was the case because the guidelines were no more than weighted averages for particular skills in the economy. Moreover, the communes were not impartial overseers when it came to the implementation of the guidelines. Very often the enterprise and the commune had a common interest in attracting additional labor; and if wage rates were too low to do this, the commune looked the other way when enterprises upgraded workers into skill levels for which they had no formal qualifications.[6]

All in all, up until 1961 state control was still quite substantial in the field of income distribution. Through a differentiated tax system for different industries, and even for different enterprises, the state was able to control both the size of the wage fund and its distribution. It managed to do this by charging a progressive tax on the wage fund exceeding the standard established wage fund,[7] and by using direct administrative means such as the establishment of a minimum wage and special guidelines for skill differentiation. Furthermore, particularly after the abolishment of the AF rate system, the state was also able to control the proportions of the wage fund, accumulation, and collective consumption via the so-called "trade union agreements." Agreements were hammered out between the trade unions and the enterprise concerning the ratio of the full wage fund to internal funds; a sort of average norm was also established for the socialized economy. Branches and enterprises with low levels of average wages, below the national average, were allowed to have a ratio of the wage fund to internal funds that was higher than the national average, while enterprises in branches with high levels of average wages could have a ratio lower than the national average. This measure was intended to ensure a reasonable amount of self-financed accumulation and collective consumption, and to reduce interbranch and interfirm wage differences.

Despite the implementation of these policies, the period of "formal" self-management, characterized by strong state intervention in income distribution, gradually came to an end. The first important event signaling the advent of serious changes was the debate at the First Congress of Workers' Councils in 1957, which demanded greater enterprise discretion over income distribution. The congress reiterated the ideological tenet that wage labor is not compatible with a genuine self-management system, and demanded that the workers' collective of an enterprise should have full control over all the net income and divide it in accordance with its preferences. The division of income into wages and profit was considered appropriate only for capitalist and etatist wage-labor relations.

But the demands of the First Congress of Workers' Councils were met only halfway. In 1958 the income distribution system was partially changed to conform to the Congress's requirements. The enterprise income was treated as a single whole and was distributed by the workers' council into wages and internal funds. However, wage rate schedules remained and were still subject to approval by local authorities and trade unions. The difference between net income and ''accounting wages'' (now called minimum personal income) was progressively taxed, as were wages in excess of certain limits over basic pay (as before).

The introduction of these half-measures did not meet with the expected general approval, and in 1961, as a part of a broader reform policy, the distribution pattern was overhauled once again. Trade union control over the division of enterprise net income was ended, and the determination of wage rates was entrusted entirely to the workers' councils. Progressive taxes on profits and excess wages were abolished, and instead, a 15% flat tax rate was levied on any net income above the minimum personal income. This tax on profit was itself abolished in 1965, and in its place a 13% flat rate payroll tax was levied on the full wage fund. Thereafter, employees' personal income and a capital charge on fixed assets[8] became the major objects of taxation.

By 1961 outside direct interference in all aspects of enterprise income distribution had been formally abolished. The only guideline left for the enterprise to follow was the minimum wage established by the federal government. The greater independence of the enterprise, both over income distribution and over the disposition of fixed assets (achieved in 1954), set the stage, as Horvat put it,[9] for a genuine market economy.

But the claim that the category of wages had been abolished in Yugoslavia was more an ideal than a reality. Although after 1961 the central statistical office stopped publishing statistical data for fixed and variable wages, replacing them with data on full wages (in conformity with the ideas of self-management), in their own accounting practices the enterprises continued to use a two-wage system, treating fixed wages as a cost deducted from gross income while variable wages were deducted from profit. What managers and workers receive as an advance on their personal income during the current operation of production is nothing else but a fixed wage. What they receive at the end of the year, or when the final income statement of the enterprise is ready, is no more than a variable wage—a sort of bonus, usually representing a small fraction of their total wages.

The reforms of 1965-1972/74

Lack of success in implementing the 1961 reforms prompted the more radical and consistent reforms of 1965. But as far as the distribution system is concerned, the economic liberalization phase started earlier than it did for other elements of the system. As mentioned, the enterprises were given more discretion over the distribution of income and wage differentials in 1961. This liberalization in the field of income distribution produced an abrupt increase in wages far in excess of labor productivity, leading to a typical cost-push inflation. Although the reforms of 1965 regarding distributional matters were not as fundamental as the reforms affecting other aspects of the economic system (such as foreign trade, prices, banking and credit, etc.), they nevertheless increased the degree of freedom the enterprise enjoyed over the size of personal income and its distribution. More precisely: progressive taxation was abolished; the flat payroll tax rate was reduced from 13% in 1961 to 10% in 1965; and the enterprise contribution out of net profit (after taxation) to the federal investment fund was abolished.[10] At the same time the producers' turnover tax, levied on about 250 products and collected at the enterprise level out of gross receipts, was replaced by a sales tax levied on consumer goods in retail trade.

As a result of all these measures the share of net income left in the enterprise rose dramatically, from the already substantially increased share of about 50% in 1961 to 66% in 1965. Under the new arrangement enterprises not only had more formal discretion over the distribution of their income, they also had more income at their disposal for investment and other purposes. The only formal restriction on distribution of incomes was the statutory federal minimum wage. There was also a sort of unwritten law recommending the increase of personal income (the combined fixed and variable wage) *pari passu* with labor productivity, the intent being to avoid inflation in this manner.[11]

For their part, the trade unions—having in mind the lingering experience of wage increases exceeding the level of labor productivity, and their loss of effective control over income distribution in 1961—strongly pushed the idea of linking wage increases with increases in labor productivity. This principle was widely accepted in 1965,[12] and for the economy as a whole it was quite reasonable. But for particular enterprises it was not. Labor productivity had risen at different rates in different industries due to their very nature. Hence, wages differed substantially between branches and enterprises, and even the differentials for the same job in different enterprises had increased substantially. This prompted pressures from the less fortunate enterprises to catch up with the wage rates of the more prosperous enterprises. In response to these pressures, wage increases in the economy after 1965 outstripped increases in labor productivity—with inflationary consequences. The catch-up process diverted large sums of money to personal incomes at the expense of internal savings, leaving the enterprises more dependent on bank credit to finance investment.

In the early 1970s important changes took place in the system as a whole. Constitutional amendments in 1970 prepared the way for the evolution of the so-called associated labor concept. These changes were expressed in a mature form in the new constitution of 1974 and the Associated Labor Act of 1976.

The years 1971-1974 were a transitional period from one concept of self-management to another. To a large extent the introduction of the associated labor concept rejected two important pillars of the socialist market economy: (a) the market mechanism as the basic mechanism of allocation and coordination of resources; and (b) macroeconomic policies and indicative planning as tools of indirect regulation of economic activities.[13] These two basic elements of the system were now to be replaced by a mechanism of contractual planning (self-management agreements and, in macro planning, social compacts), in order to reduce the role of spontaneous market forces and widen the planning process beyond traditional macro planning.

A combination of socioeconomic factors explains the change of course in the 1970s. The economic reforms of 1965 were considered a failure by the elite in power and by some academic economists. In addition to increased inequalities, those reforms had given rise to several other negative phenomena in the economy. To mention only a few: a slowdown of growth with an increase in unemployment; an increase of inflationary pressures, attributable to the enterprises' greater discretion over the distribution of income; a lack of improvement in the balance of payment, contrary to initial expectations; massive abuse of the taxation system; an increase in corruption; and a considerable widening of inequalities between regions and sectors, with all the political tensions that entails.

Student unrest in 1968 and rising nationalist antagonisms were manifestations of social instability and discontent. But the change of course in the 1970s was not only linked with the economic failures of the reforms. The erosion of the communist party's political power, perceived as a product of marketization of the economy, was another impetus to the new changes. The reforms of 1965 had increased the power of the managerial strata by undermining workers' control in the enterprises, but they also threatened to deprive the party bureaucracy of its political control and to remove it from the decision-making process. Mencinger, reflecting on these developments, wrote: "The constitutional changes became inevitable if the political basis of the system was to be saved. The market proved socially and politically less neutral than it is assumed in the traditional Langean theory of the socialist market economy."[14]

The underlying philosophy of the changes in the 1970s was that self-managed enterprises based on social property would promote cooperation rather than competition among economic units. Hence, the free play of spontaneous market forces would be restrained (but not abolished). New instruments of coordination were to be developed; namely, contractual planning, especially self-managed agreements and social compacts.

According to Mencinger,[15] the new planning system can be summarized as follows:

(a) planning involves all relevant organizations and requires their active participation; it also carries a legal obligation for all decision-making units;

(b) planning consists of microeconomic planning—referred to as self-managed planning of economic units—and macroeconomic planning—referred to as social planning of sociopolitical communities, e.g., between governments on different levels, between government agents on any level and other agents in the economy including enterprises, economic chambers, trade unions, and SMAI (self-management and associations of interests);

(c) planning involves the obligatory exchange of information by all economic units. Coordination is legally binding for priority sectors and their enterprises;

(d) planning is a continued process carried out by all planning agents. The five-year plan is the basic tool of planning.

Agreements were to serve as a mechanism of communication replacing direct intervention of planning bodies and reliance on price and quantity signals. These agreements encompassed not only quantities and prices, etc., but also common investment ventures (pooling resources). It was hoped that direct contractual pooling of resources for investment projects would improve the mobility of capital and encourage the distribution of investable funds between surplus and deficit enterprises without the involvement of the banking system, which was ideologically and politically suspect. Hence, contracts were seen as a substitute for a capital market that would solve the problem of capital mobility. The old idea prevailing in socialist economics, that the market mechanism is a bad allocator of investment goods (because at the moment of decision making there is no information about future prices and costs), was invoked. In other words, current prices reflected current scarcities; and since the market could not provide information about future scarcities, it could not guarantee an optimal solution.

Although interfirm competition was still considered desirable, especially in the investment process, contractual planning was meant to encourage *ex ante* competition for funds, before and not after the factories were built, something rather usual for a free market system. When negotiations among trade unions, economic chambers, and sociopolitical communities were completed, the agreed investment targets were to be incorporated in some 240 social agreements (one for each of the thirty sectors in each of the six republics and two autonomous provinces). The objective of this kind of planning was to achieve an *ex ante* structure of future capacities and to avoid duplication. Corresponding social agreements were then concluded on prices: import and export, personal incomes, employment, and so on. Within the framework of social agreements between branches and sectors under the auspices of the economic chambers, firms competed for the right to implement the program, and interfirm self-management agreements were subsequently concluded.

Although formally only priority sectors were legally obliged to conclude social agreements, due to a variety of pressures all sectors were doing so. The only difference was that in the case of priority sectors the banks were obliged to ensure them the needed resources.

Contractual planning of this kind enabled the federal authorities to intervene on a permanent basis in the formulation and implementation of macro-objectives. However, the instruments available to the federal government for the regulation of money supply, aggregate demand, prices, wages, import and export were very few and unsophisticated. The federation was stripped of most of its fiscal powers after 1965. The enterprise charge on enterprise business funds and federal taxes on private incomes were abolished, and the federal turnover tax was to be handed over to the republics. Only custom duties, together with a few other minor sources of income, remained in federal hands. Although the federal government continued to be responsible for the administration of the accelerated development fund for the underdeveloped regions, the republics bore the burden of financing it.

The federal government had henceforth to rely on republican contributions and on borrowing to finance most of its activities, and the consent of the republics was required even with respect to those functions for which the federal government was still responsible; e.g., the five-year plan, monetary policy, foreign currency and external trade matters, and even the federal budget itself.

The process of weakening the market character of the economy was also accompanied by a more egalitarian distribution policy. In view of serious student unrest and nationalistic fervor in some regions, the state had decided that the greater dispersion of income was not desirable, and serious steps were taken to limit the rights of enterprises to distribute income. The anti-laissez-faire faction won the day, although not without opposition. By 1972 the state organs had imposed controls over the distribution of income per worker between personal income and internal funds, and over the distribution of net personal income among employees. In some republics, formulas or principles were established regulating the distribution between personal income and internal funds. Although these formulas were somewhat different in different republics, they imposed a new and common logic: those enterprises that had higher than average net incomes per worker had to allocate a higher percentage to internal funds (savings, consumption funds, reserves) and a lower percentage to personal incomes, whereas enterprises with net incomes per worker below the average had to do the opposite.[16] As a result, differences in personal incomes per worker between enterprises and branches declined in comparison with the years of the post-1965 reform.

As far as skill differentials were concerned, all enterprises received a sort of a guideline regarding the distribution of personal incomes among employees. In each firm the maximum average personal income per worker in each skill category was to be kept in some relation to the average personal income of unskilled workers (e.g., the maximum personal income of the highest skill category could not be larger on the average than three times that for the unskilled category). This measure allowed the state authorities to control the differentials between groups, professions, and skills. The above-mentioned formulas and guidelines were implemented via social contracts signed by the enterprises, towns, regions, etc. It hardly need be pointed out here that, given a distributional pattern where increases in net income per worker lead only to modest increases in personal incomes, workers within the enterprise will try to direct more funds to collective consumption, irrespective of cost considerations, in order to compensate themselves for the pecuniary loss with nonpecuniary benefits.

The new principles and guidelines were short-lived and never seriously implemented. Social contracts became a subject of constant political negotiation, and some contracts were never enforced.

Social planning

In 1974 the new constitution, and two years later the Associated Labor Act (1976), resulted in a far-reaching regional decentralization which wiped out all the above-mentioned guidelines and formulas established by the federal government. Under the new constitution, republics and autonomous provinces became *de facto* nearly sovereign states. All regulations in the field of income distribution became the prerogative of each republic. Because of these changes, distributional regulations were hereafter different in the various republics and provinces. In some republics, for example, an additional factor determining the distribution of net income was introduced; namely, the proportion of personal income was linked not only with the net income per worker but also with the ratio of savings to capital assets (S/K). Enterprises with above-average net incomes per worker have the right to allocate a larger part of their total net income to personal income, provided that their capital stock will grow at a rate higher than the average in the republic. By and large, in most republics after 1975 the only constraint on income distribution by the enterprises was the minimum net personal income, calculated as a fraction of the average net personal income established by republican authorities. In most cases a maximum net personal income ceiling was abolished. In fact, after 1975 very few guidelines regulating interbranch and skill differentials remained; it was left to the discretion of each republic to decide how much and in what way to meddle in these differentials.

But while the federal government was deprived of its right to intervene in these fields, the republics were not. Indeed, this principle applies not only to income distribution but also to the decision-making process in other spheres of social and economic life.

The scope of the republican authorities' discretion over income distribution is well illustrated by the dissimilarity of their interbranch and intersectoral structures of personal income and rates of accumulation, as the result of independent distribution policies including tax policies.[17] Likewise, comparisons of the tax structures in different republics have shown great dissimilarities in the allocation of tax funds for different social purposes.[18] Making the situation even more heterogeneous is the fact that the absolute amount of taxes collected by each republic is more or less proportional to the gross personal income. Hence, the more affluent republics with, on the average, higher gross personal incomes automatically have more taxes at their disposal, and this has a very substantial impact on the level and quality of schooling, health care, and other social services offered in each republic. This situation is indeed unusual. Even the most decentralized system in the capitalist world has some equalization programs as far as social benefits are concerned; the authorities try to equalize the funding of basic education, basic health care, etc., in different regions and locations. In the case of Yugoslavia, however, the republics' aversion to any type of federal centralization goes so far as to oppose the operation of a common energy system or communication system. But it is revealing that, for example, Slovenia has implemented a highly centralized energy system. It seems that for some republics, usually the most prosperous ones, state hands-off policies are desirable only where the federation is concerned; in their own ''house'' republican authorities do not hesitate to impose strong centralized measures.[19]

The new constitution of 1974, in an attempt to limit the role of administrative orders, made it obligatory for all enterprises to sign social compacts[20] indicating their distribution policy, in accordance with general social objectives. But these social agreements are very vague and general and, more importantly, are not compulsory. Therefore they could not be, and they have not been, enforced by the state, and ultimately the enterprises have had full discretion over the division of their total net income. This leads to a situation in which many enterprises in the less prosperous republics have not been able to accumulate adequate savings after allocating net income for personal needs.

What kind of general assessment can be made of this new system? Theoretically the new planning system is highly attractive because it promises an *ex ante* equilibrium solution, introducing elements of indicative and direct planning, and encouraging a broad exchange of information.[21] Ideologically the new planning system has a number of attractions as well. It cannot be accused of increasing bureaucratic intervention, and it appears as favorable to participatory democracy. In other words, the compulsive elements of the system are skillfully hidden behind the impression that the social agreements are not obligatory.[22]

In reality, however, the system introduced in the 1970s has proven a failure. Neither of its major sociopolitical goals were achieved. The new laws regulating the behavior of units in the areas of income distribution, price information, and foreign trade were in most cases abolished in favor of administrative measures. Most of the elements of the system were inoperative or irrelevant for economic activities. For example, the system of contractual planning could not be implemented. Such an all-embracing planning system would have required the negotiation of an enormous number of plans. In addition, the system was overloaded with institutions, some of which were useless. In general the blueprint of the system became inoperative or produced undesirable results requiring government intervention to the extent that, gradually, it was replaced by a quasi-administrative system. The system introduced in the 1970s was based on ideological perception of reality which, among other things, miscalculated future expectations and was not very realistic.

The current crisis

The economic crisis that hit Yugoslavia around 1980 forced the government to rethink certain aspects of the changes introduced in the 1970s. There was an urgent need for a long-term program to revitalize the economy. To this end the Federal Social Council, created at the beginning of 1982 (called the Kraigher Commission after its chairman, a prominent high-ranking government official dealing with economic problems), was entrusted with working out a stabilization program. In July 1983 the Commission's program was officially adopted by the Federal Assembly and became state policy. This huge, four-volume government document, called the "Long-Term Program of Economic Stabilization," boils down to four points.

(1) Yugoslavia should concentrate on production where it has a comparative advantage, and should avoid the existing practice of producing nearly everything domestically.

(2) The process of defederalization had gone too far. Yugoslavia resembled a confederation rather than a federation. More power should be given to the federal bodies in the field of macroeconomic planning and general economic policy.[23]

(3) A unitary market should be established, with more mobility of labor and capital.

(4) The income of successful enterprises should not be redistributed in favor of less successful ones. Enterprises must bear the consequences of their activities. The prevailing practice of socializing risk should be stopped. Certain changes should be introduced in the principle of dividing the net income of the enterprise. More precisely, it was recommended that from January 1985, an enterprise would have the right to pay out personal incomes above the (republic)

average only if its rate of accumulation (the ratio of savings to the capital stock, or S/K) was above the average rate in the republic. The purpose of this measure was to make accumulation the priority in distribution, rather than a residual after personal incomes had been paid out, as had often been the practice.

There are some difficulties, however, in implementing this last principle. Enterprises with low levels of net income per worker are usually those enterprises with low capital intensity levels (K/L), and for them to increase the ratio of savings to the capital stock above the republic average is very difficult, because this ratio (S/K) is linked with the degree of capital intensity. Hence, as far as personal incomes are concerned, enterprises with poorer performances will be penalized in comparison with the previous system.

The main orientation of the new program is quite clear: more reliance on the market mechanism and a reduction in the institutions of contractual planning.[24]

But from the very beginning this program faced strong opposition from many quarters, and most of its recommendations, at least up to 1989, have not been implemented. The prolonged crisis since 1983 has again put on the agenda a broad discussion how to overcome the crisis in Yugoslavia. In April 1987 the federal government issued for public discussion a document called the "Theses on the Further Improvement of the Economic System" (*Teze za dalju dogradnju privrednog sistema*), and followed in October 1988 by introducing new legislative proposals in the federal parliament. One of the characteristics of these documents is that they (like the stabilization program of 1983) are very rich in generalities but vague on specifics. This is particularly evident when it comes to questions of property relations and markets for capital and labor. What is more, some ideas and proposals are just a repetition of previous programs. Nevertheless, certain points in these federal documents represent some progress in comparison with previous government proposals and therefore merit attention. The gist of these documents can be summarized in the following points.

(1) Enterprises should be allowed to issue a larger variety of bonds and shares with flexible and fixed returns. However, shareholders will not have voting rights or control over management decisions.

(2) Yugoslav citizens should be allowed, just like foreigners, to

invest their savings in their own firms or create partnership firms.

(3) Investors should receive not, as before, a fixed interest, but a share in the extra income created by the investment in proportion to its contribution of resources. This measure is intended to encourage the pooling of resources by self-managed enterprises.

(4) Liberalization of the restrictions on transfer of profits abroad, as well as some widening of the property rights of foreign capital owners, in order to encourage the inflow of foreign capital and joint ventures.

(5) Leasing (time-sharing) the capacities of some small enterprises in manufacturing and services to foreigners and Yugoslav citizens for a certain specified period of time. (Up to now this has been permitted only in the tourism sector.)

(6) The limits on landholdings (currently 10 hectares, or 25 acres) should be raised. A proposal was introduced in the federal parliament in October 1988 to increase landholding limits to 30 hectares. Comparable increases were to apply to other forms of private property as well.

(7) The ''Theses on the Further Improvement of the Economic System,'' published in April 1987, proposed the reestablishment of a capital charge reflecting the scarcity of capital. However, no specific suggestions about the magnitude of the capital charge were made.

(8) Introduction of a ''bonus'' linked to the number of years a worker has been employed in a firm. This is a sort of interest on the savings the worker has provided to the enterprise, and is to be paid annually even when the employee leaves the enterprise. The purpose of this ''bonus'' is intended to encourage workers to increase internal savings in the enterprise and make them more interested not only in the size of personal income but also in the accumulation of capital stock in the enterprise.

(9) At the beginning of October 1988 the government also brought before the federal parliament proposed legislation on socioeconomic planning. This proposal asked for a dramatic reduction of the scope of economic development planning. The obligation to work out plans would be limited only to a few sectors of basic importance such as energy, railroads, and communications. Enterprises in the production sphere should be given the responsibility of deciding whether a plan was needed. Even more radical is a proposal to abolish the compli-

cated and time-consuming procedure of self-management agreements at all levels of the economic system, which have been the basis for the planning process up to the present. In place of this network of planning, the federal government proposed a strengthening of federal macroeconomic instruments capable of influencing economic decisions via the market.

(10) The document also advocated granting managers more responsibility in the supervision of employees and more discretion to discipline workers for bad performance. But the proposal stops short of giving managers the right to fire employees and does not suggest a transition to a full-fledged labor market.

(11) A more consistent fiscal system for the whole country. Certain taxes should be equalized in all republics. The old practice of nearly total decentralization of taxes was harmful to the unity of the country and should be abolished. (It should be noted here that in October 1988 a tax policy proposal to be implemented on the federal level was introduced, but was vetoed by the republic of Slovenia.)

Although, at least on paper, there is some consensus among republics for the implementation of some of these proposals, in reality such prospects are rather remote. There seems to be a sort of equilibrium between those for and those against the implementation of these changes, and the result has been a political stalemate. The prosperous republics support the more market-oriented proposals but refuse to grant more power to the federation. The poorer regions do not object to a stronger role for the federal government in macroeconomic policy, but they oppose far-reaching marketization of the economy, fearing that this would threaten the influx of resources from the central fund for less developed regions and that they would lose out in competition with the stronger republics. A lack of common interest and perception about the fundamental problems mentioned above does not make the prospects very bright for breaking the stalemate and implementing the changes proposed by the federal government. And it should not be surprising that well-entrenched forces and institutions in the republics are not disposed to give up powers they have held since the introduction of the 1974 constitution. It may well be that a new constitution limiting the rights of the republics would be required for most of these proposals to be implemented.

For the time being the stalemate between the forces of federation and the republics continues, hindering major reforms. The dramatic events in Yugoslavia in the autumn of 1988, when a wave of strikes forced the resignations of the elites in some republics, did not change this stalemate.

To conclude, our survey of changes in the Yugoslav system shows that the self-managed system of income distribution has evolved gradually, as part of a historical process. The enterprises gained independent control over income distribution and income differentials as a result of the reforms of 1961 and 1965. In this realm, the principles of a self-managed market economy were firmly established. Nevertheless, deviations from this laissez-faire situation were not infrequent. With varying degrees of intensity and success, the state has intervened directly in the pattern of income distribution, encroaching on the logic of a self-managed system.

CHAPTER II

Statistical Analysis

Having reviewed the history of income distribution policies in postwar Yugoslavia,[1] we will now attempt to give a detailed statistical account of pay dispersion for the period 1964 to 1983.[2]

The Dispersion of Personal Incomes

The relative dispersion of earnings in the socialized sector of Yugoslavia in general, and in the socialized industries in particular (shown in Table 1, following, and Appendix Table A), allows us to draw the following conclusions:

(1) By all the measures of inequality used here, the overall relative dispersion of pay has slightly declined in Yugoslavia in the period under investigation; but the noted changes are not substantial. The decline in relative dispersion is substantial only at the extremes of the distributional spectrum (P_{99}/P_1) and (P_{98}/P_2), corresponding to higher and lower income groups. This declining trend is less pronounced if we use the more synthetic Gini coefficients or the decile ratio (P_{90}/P_{10}). Although it is difficult to distinguish clear-cut subperiods of change, one stands out very distinctly: the period of 1964-1969, when we observe a substantial increase in relative dispersion of personal income. These years coincide with the laissez-faire period in Yugoslavia. This period comes to an end in 1971, and soon thereafter a decline of income inequality takes place. This decline intensifies in the 1980s, probably as a result of the economic crisis.

(2) The relative dispersion of personal incomes is larger in the nonmaterial than in the material production sphere, although the overall changes are more or less the same in both spheres. The higher levels of inequality in the nonmaterial sphere are a reflection of the special privileges enjoyed by the upper echelons of the administration and the top party apparatus on the one hand, and the very low pay received by clerical personnel on the other.[3] In no other sector of the socialized economy did the lowest-paid 1% and 2% of workers

receive such a small part of the median as in the nonmaterial sphere. From this point of view Yugoslavia is not different from other East European countries. There are, however, some important differences between Yugoslavia and the Comecon countries as far as the nonmaterial sphere is concerned, and these should be pointed out. Yugoslavia is the only country where average pay is higher in the nonmaterial than in the material sphere. In the Soviet Union, for example, the earnings in the nonmaterial sphere are only 80% of those in the material sphere, whereas in Yugoslavia this ratio oscillates between 104% and 120% (see mean and median in Table 1). What is even more important, in the Comecon countries in general, the low average wages in the nonmaterial production sector are mainly the result of very low wages—much below the average—in the health, education, and cultural sectors. In Yugoslavia this is not the case. The wages in these sectors are approximately equal to the average of the socialized sector—which is obviously more reasonable.

(3) The inequality of pay in industry is smaller than in the socialized sector, but the trend of change is more or less the same: an increase of inequality after the reform of 1965, and a decline in the postreform years. The slightly higher level of inequality in the whole socialized sector than in industry reflects the influence of the higher relative dispersion in the nonmaterial sphere and some sectors of the material production sphere, especially construction.

(4) Although frequency distribution data for the republics and autonomous provinces are available only for the period 1964-1976, computed measures of dispersion allow us to conclude that there was a decline in the relative dispersion of pay in all the republics and provinces except Vojvodina. The decline was very dramatic in Kosovo, the most backward region of the country, to the point where this autonomous province moved from the position of a leader in inequality of pay in 1964, to a relative dispersion of net personal income equal to the national average in 1976. In all the republics and provinces except Kosovo, we observe, as in the federation in total, an increase in relative dispersion of personal income after the 1965 reform, but this lasted only for a very short time. As early as 1969-71, with some variation in different republics, the relative dispersion of pay started to decline, and in some areas by 1976 it reached lower levels of dispersion than in 1964.

Table 1

Distribution of Net Personal Income in the Socialized Sector of Yugoslavia, 1964–1983 (measures of dispersion)

Yugoslavia Total

	1964	1966	1967	1969	1971	1972	1973	1974
P_1	0.40	0.35	0.35	0.38	0.43	0.45	0.46	0.48
P_2	0.46	0.44	0.42	0.46	0.47	0.49	0.50	0.52
P_5	0.54	0.53	0.52	0.53	0.54	0.56	0.57	0.58
P_{10}	0.62	0.61	0.60	0.61	0.62	0.63	0.63	0.65
P_{15}	0.67	0.67	0.66	0.66	0.67	0.68	0.69	0.70
P_{25}	0.77	0.77	0.76	0.77	0.77	0.78	0.78	0.79
P_{75}	1.32	1.31	1.32	1.32	1.32	1.29	1.29	1.29
P_{85}	1.55	1.52	1.56	1.57	1.54	1.52	1.53	1.51
P_{90}	1.73	1.70	1.75	1.77	1.74	1.73	1.72	1.68
P_{95}	2.05	2.03	2.09	2.13	2.12	2.06	2.05	1.99
P_{98}	2.50	2.47	2.62	2.69	2.60	2.53	2.48	2.46
P_{99}	2.87	2.82	3.01	3.14	3.01	2.95	2.81	2.90
Median (M)	409.9	661.4	693.07	873.3	1,275.3	1,514.9	1,752.5	2,227.7
Mean (x̄)	452.9	724.4	763.6	973.5	1,418.3	1,675.2	1,934.7	2,457.5
$P_{99}{:}P_1$	7.09	8.14	8.66	8.33	7.00	6.59	6.15	6.11
$P_{98}{:}P_2$	5.42	5.66	6.18	5.88	5.50	5.14	4.96	4.78
$P_{95}{:}P_5$	3.80	3.85	4.05	4.00	3.92	3.67	3.62	3.43
$P_{90}{:}P_{10}$	2.81	2.80	2.91	2.92	2.82	2.74	2.70	2.60
$P_{85}{:}P_{15}$	2.29	2.27	2.36	2.36	2.29	2.23	2.22	2.16
$Q_3{:}Q_1$	1.71	1.70	1.74	1.73	1.72	1.67	1.65	1.64
$Q_3{-}Q_1/M$	0.54	0.54	0.56	0.56	0.55	0.52	0.51	0.51
(V)	45.97	45.6	46.8	47.7	47.04	45.4	44.3	43.03
Gini	0.23	0.23	0.24	0.24	0.23	0.23	0.22	0.21

	1975	1976	1978	1979	1980	1981	1982	1983
P_1	0.46	0.46	0.44	0.45	0.45	0.45	0.46	0.45
P_2	0.51	0.50	0.49	0.49	0.49	0.49	0.51	0.49
P_5	0.57	0.57	0.56	0.56	0.56	0.56	0.57	0.56
P_{10}	0.64	0.63	0.63	0.63	0.63	0.63	0.64	0.63
P_{15}	0.69	0.68	0.69	0.69	0.68	0.69	0.70	0.68
P_{25}	0.78	0.78	0.78	0.78	0.77	0.79	0.79	0.79
P_{75}	1.30	1.29	1.31	1.32	1.29	1.28	1.29	1.28
P_{85}	1.50	1.49	1.53	1.53	1.50	1.48	1.49	1.48
P_{90}	1.67	1.65	1.70	1.71	1.65	1.65	1.65	1.65
P_{95}	1.96	1.97	2.02	2.03	1.97	1.90	1.93	1.99
P_{98}	2.45	2.45	2.48	2.51	2.38	2.18	2.40	2.43
P_{99}	2.87	2.83	2.86	2.83	2.64	2.32	2.69	2.71
Median	2,787.1	3,252.5	5,053.5	5,445.5	6,851.5	9,168.3	11,604.0	14,851.5
Mean ($\bar{x}$)	3,045.4	3,547.1	4,594.1	6,004.6	7,427.0	9,808.2	1,262.6	16,134.5
$P_{99}:P_1$	6.20	6.09	6.44	6.29	5.85	5.16	5.81	5.98
$P_{98}:P_2$	4.83	4.87	5.07	5.08	4.87	4.43	4.74	4.94
$P_{95}:P_5$	3.43	3.49	3.62	3.63	3.54	3.42	3.38	3.56
$P_{90}:P_{10}$	2.61	2.64	2.70	2.70	2.64	2.60	2.56	2.62
$P_{85}:P_{15}$	2.18	2.17	2.23	2.23	2.20	2.13	2.14	2.16
$Q_3:Q_1$	1.66	1.64	1.67	1.69	1.68	1.62	1.64	1.63
Q_3-Q_1/M	0.51	0.50	0.52	0.54	0.52	0.49	0.50	0.49
(V)	42.90	42.7	43.65	43.07	41.10	38.02	40.7	41.42
Gini	0.21	0.21	0.22	0.22	0.21	0.20	0.21	0.21

Table 1 (continued)

Nonmaterial Sphere

	1964	1966	1967	1969	1971	1972	1973	1974
P_1	0.40	0.33	0.37	0.41	0.41	0.43	0.43	0.45
P_2	0.40	0.41	0.43	0.45	0.46	0.47	0.47	0.49
P_5	0.51	0.51	0.52	0.52	0.52	0.53	0.54	0.55
P_{10}	0.59	0.60	0.60	0.60	0.60	0.60	0.61	0.62
P_{15}	0.65	0.66	0.66	0.67	0.67	0.66	0.68	0.68
P_{25}	0.77	0.78	0.78	0.79	0.78	0.78	0.79	0.80
P_{75}	1.30	1.27	1.28	1.31	1.30	1.28	1.31	1.29
P_{85}	1.54	1.50	1.51	1.57	1.55	1.54	1.56	1.54
P_{90}	1.75	1.69	1.72	1.79	1.79	1.75	1.78	1.73
P_{95}	2.11	2.03	2.12	2.17	2.14	2.10	2.10	2.07
P_{98}	2.61	2.49	2.58	2.72	2.64	2.59	2.51	2.60
P_{99}	3.05	2.87	2.86	3.10	3.12	2.99	2.93	3.02
Median	485.9	737.6	799.0	982.2	1,427.7	1,728.7	1,976.2	2,455.5
Mean ($\bar{x}$)	535.7	803.9	874.8	1,096.2	1,588.2	1,907.1	2,198.5	2,715.4
P_{99}:P_1	7.64	8.78	7.77	7.62	7.53	6.91	6.77	6.70
P_{98}:P_2	5.93	6.12	5.94	6.05	5.81	5.47	5.32	5.34
P_{95}:P_5	4.13	3.98	4.06	4.17	4.10	3.95	3.92	3.80
P_{90}:P_{10}	2.98	2.82	2.88	2.98	2.98	2.93	2.91	2.81
P_{85}:P_{15}	2.36	2.26	2.29	2.33	2.32	2.32	2.30	2.24
Q_3:Q_1	1.68	1.64	1.63	1.65	1.66	1.64	1.64	1.65
Q_3–Q_1/M	0.53	0.50	0.49	0.52	0.52	0.50	0.51	0.49
(V)	47.3	45.9	44.8	47.0	47.5	46.1	45.6	44.9
Gini	0.24	0.23	0.23	0.24	0.24	0.23	0.23	0.22

	1975	1976	1978	1979	1980	1981	1982	1983
P_1	0.45	0.45	0.43	0.43	0.43	0.44	0.45	0.45
P_2	0.48	0.48	0.47	0.46	0.46	0.47	0.48	0.48
P_5	0.54	0.54	0.53	0.53	0.53	0.54	0.54	0.54
P_{10}	0.61	0.61	0.60	0.60	0.60	0.61	0.62	0.61
P_{15}	0.67	0.68	0.67	0.67	0.67	0.68	0.68	0.68
P_{25}	0.80	0.80	0.79	0.77	0.78	0.79	0.79	0.79
P_{75}	1.28	1.28	1.30	1.31	1.30	1.28	1.29	1.28
P_{85}	1.52	1.53	1.54	1.53	1.53	1.49	1.52	1.50
P_{90}	1.71	1.74	1.74	1.72	1.70	1.65	1.71	1.71
P_{95}	2.08	2.09	2.08	2.05	2.02	1.89	2.05	2.09
P_{98}	2.62	2.62	2.58	2.46	2.36	2.12	2.46	2.49
P_{99}	2.97	2.96	2.94	2.69	2.53	2.23	2.71	2.73
Median (M)	3,104.0	3,633.7	5,271.8	6,227.7	7,485.2	9,634.0	12,297.0	15,307.0
Mean (X̄)	3,419.0	4,016.1	5,764.4	6,802.8	8,127.9	10,279.5	13,452.0	16,747.0
P_{99}:P_1	6.65	6.64	6.87	6.30	5.88	5.09	6.04	6.08
P_{98}:P_2	5.44	5.48	5.54	5.34	5.08	4.48	5.10	5.16
P_{95}:P_5	3.85	3.90	3.93	3.89	3.85	3.52	3.76	3.86
P_{90}:P_{10}	2.82	2.84	2.88	2.84	2.82	2.69	2.77	2.80
P_{85}:P_{15}	2.25	2.23	2.29	2.29	2.30	2.19	2.22	2.23
Q_3:Q_1	1.62	1.61	1.66	1.69	1.67	1.63	1.65	1.63
Q_3–Q_1/M	0.49	0.49	0.52	0.53	0.52	0.49	0.51	0.50
(V)	44.5	44.7	44.7	42.9	41.5	38.0	42.2	42.8
Gini	0.22	0.22	0.23	0.22	0.22	0.20	0.22	0.22

Table 1 (continued)

Industry

	1964	1966	1967	1969	1971	1972	1973	1974
P_1	0.42	0.36	0.35	0.39	0.46	0.47	0.48	0.48
P_2	0.47	0.44	0.44	0.47	0.50	0.51	0.52	0.52
P_5	0.55	0.54	0.53	0.55	0.56	0.58	0.58	0.59
P_{10}	0.62	0.62	0.60	0.62	0.63	0.65	0.65	0.66
P_{15}	0.68	0.68	0.66	0.68	0.69	0.70	0.70	0.71
P_{25}	0.77	0.77	0.76	0.77	0.78	0.79	0.79	0.80
P_{75}	1.33	1.32	1.34	1.33	1.32	1.29	1.28	1.30
P_{85}	1.56	1.55	1.58	1.56	1.54	1.50	1.50	1.50
P_{90}	1.74	1.72	1.77	1.75	1.71	1.69	1.68	1.66
P_{95}	2.05	2.02	2.10	2.09	2.06	2.01	1.98	1.93
P_{98}	2.45	2.43	2.63	2.60	2.54	2.46	2.38	2.33
P_{99}	2.81	2.77	3.05	3.07	2.91	2.77	2.72	2.69
Median (M)	408.7	638.6	657.4	843.6	1,227.7	1,441.6	1,681.2	2,188.1
Mean (x̄)	379.3	704.7	730.6	940.0	1,365.7	1,588.9	1,846.1	2,402.8
$P_{99}{:}P_1$	6.64	7.71	8.74	7.86	6.34	5.96	5.71	5.56
$P_{98}{:}P_2$	5.19	5.50	6.00	5.49	5.13	4.83	4.59	4.47
$P_{95}{:}P_5$	3.76	3.78	3.99	3.82	3.66	3.47	3.39	3.27
$P_{90}{:}P_{10}$	2.81	2.80	2.93	2.82	2.69	2.60	2.58	2.52
$P_{85}{:}P_{15}$	2.30	2.29	2.38	2.30	2.22	2.14	2.14	2.10
$Q_3{:}Q_1$	1.71	1.71	1.75	1.72	1.69	1.64	1.62	1.63
$Q_3{-}Q_1/M$	0.55	0.55	0.58	0.55	0.54	0.50	0.49	0.50
(V)	45.3	44.8	47.1	46.5	45.3	43.2	42.3	40.9
Gini	0.23	0.23	0.24	0.23	0.22	0.22	0.21	0.21

	1975	1976	1978	1979	1980	1981	1982	1983
P_1	0.46	0.47	0.44	0.45	0.45	0.46	0.46	0.45
P_2	0.51	0.51	0.49	0.50	0.49	0.49	0.50	0.49
P_5	0.58	0.57	0.56	0.57	0.56	0.57	0.58	0.57
P_{10}	0.65	0.64	0.64	0.64	0.64	0.65	0.66	0.64
P_{15}	0.70	0.69	0.69	0.69	0.69	0.70	0.71	0.69
P_{25}	0.78	0.79	0.79	0.79	0.78	0.80	0.80	0.79
P_{75}	1.29	1.29	1.29	1.31	1.28	1.26	1.28	1.28
P_{85}	1.49	1.49	1.50	1.51	1.48	1.46	1.47	1.46
P_{90}	1.65	1.64	1.66	1.66	1.62	1.61	1.61	1.62
P_{95}	1.91	1.92	1.94	1.92	1.90	1.88	1.87	1.93
P_{98}	2.29	2.29	2.30	2.37	2.33	2.16	2.28	2.39
P_{99}	2.68	2.69	2.66	2.75	2.61	2.32	2.60	2.68
Median (M)	2,718.0	3,114.0	4,356.4	5,138.6	6,333.7	9,059.4	11,346.5	14,792.0
Mean ($\bar{x}$)	2,953	3,386.5	4,742.0	5,614.6	7,144.7	9,664.6	12,256.5	16,005.0
P_{99}:P_1	5.78	5.68	6.02	6.13	5.77	5.17	5.68	5.99
P_{98}:P_2	4.50	4.50	4.68	4.73	4.73	4.39	4.50	4.83
P_{95}:P_5	3.30	3.35	3.46	3.38	3.38	3.30	3.21	3.40
P_{90}:P_{10}	2.54	2.58	2.61	2.60	2.55	2.49	2.46	2.54
P_{85}:P_{15}	2.14	2.15	2.17	2.17	2.14	2.07	2.07	2.11
Q_3:Q_1	1.65	1.63	1.64	1.66	1.65	1.58	1.61	1.61
Q_3–Q_1/M	0.51	0.50	0.50	0.52	0.51	0.47	0.48	0.49
(V)	41.2	41.1	41.5	41.4	40.1	37.2	39.2	40.4
Gini	0.21	0.21	0.21	0.21	0.21	0.19	0.20	0.21

Source: Statistical Yearbook of Yugoslavia (SGJ).

Notes: P_5, P_{25}, etc., refer to the 5th, 25th, etc., percentiles of earnings expressed as a ratio of the median, ordering wage, and salary earners from low incomes to high incomes; e.g., P_5 refers to the bottom 5% of earners and P_{95} refers to the top 5%.

Q_1 is the lower quartile; Q_3 is the upper quartile; V is the coefficient of variation (%), computed by dividing the standard deviation by the mean.

(5) Our computed data do not show any clear correlation between the stage of development of the various republics and provinces (measured in terms of national income per capita) and inequality of pay. From the statistical data presented here we can observe cases where a less developed region has a lower dispersion of pay than a more developed one, and vice versa. For example, Macedonia has a lower degree of inequality than the more developed Vojvodina, and nearly the same degree as the second most developed republic, Croatia. Montenegro and Kosovo, both very underdeveloped regions, have higher degrees of inequality of pay, however. We should not overlook the fact that the two richest republics, Slovenia and Croatia, have a relative dispersion of pay below the national average, with Slovenia having the lowest relative dispersion of pay of all the republics and provinces.

(6) At a different level of comparison, we can also suggest that the dispersion of pay in Yugoslavia is very low by Western standards, similar to the pattern found in Hungary and lower than the pattern in Poland and the USSR.[4] Evidence indicates, however, that in the long run, changes in all the socialist countries are going in the same direction; namely, there is a decline in inequality of pay. This process is more pronounced in the USSR than in Yugoslavia, which is understandable if we take into consideration that the Soviet Union started with much higher levels of inequality after the war.

This observation refers to aggregate data in which pay differences between the sexes are not taken into account. Thus a few additional points have to be registered here. Unfortunately, Yugoslav statistics (unlike the Hungarian and Polish ones) do not publish average monthly pay by sex. We can only infer from the very specific structure of female employment that there is a large gap in pay between the sexes. Women are heavily concentrated in the unskilled category of work and they are practically nonexistent in the highly skilled category. It is sufficient to point out that in 1971 more than one-third of all women were unskilled workers and only 4% were highly skilled workers.[5] Top managerial and technical jobs are virtually monopolized by men (less than 1% of all top enterprise managers are women). What is even more important, women's employment clearly remains concentrated in occupations that are viewed as natural extensions of their domestic roles: food processing, clothing/textiles, teachers in primary education, nurses, midwives, secretaries, typists, etc.[6] Considering the very high concentration of female employment in these jobs, differences in average pay between unskilled and highly skilled workers give a good approximation of the pay gap between the sexes in Yugoslavia. As can be seen from Table 2, the picture is not very encouraging. The difference was nearly 1.9:1 in 1966, and although the gap had narrowed to 1.7:1 in 1983, women's earnings are still less than 60% of men's earnings.

It is also appropriate to mention that there is a regional dimension to pay inequalities between the sexes. The more developed a region is, the higher is the participation rate of women in the labor force and the better are the job opportunities for women in industry and in other higher paid sectors. Considering the very great differences in the level of development of different republics and provinces, the participation rates of women are, as expected, dramatically different. Slovenia, the most developed republic, had a women's participation rate of nearly 41% in 1971, whereas Kosovo, the most underdeveloped region, had a rate of only 8.3%.[7] Of course, the very low participation rate of women in Kosovo is not only a result of the stage of economic development. Other factors play a role as well, and one of them is religion. The overwhelming majority of the population in Kosovo is Muslim, and religious custom and tradition dictate that women be kept at home.

Having analyzed the overall relative dispersion of personal incomes in Yugoslavia, let us investigate the structure of inequality. How have interskill, interbranch, and interregional differentials contributed to the overall relative dispersion of pay in Yugoslavia?

Interskill Differentials

As can be seen from Table 2, interskill differentials in Yugoslavia are quite small by Western standards and are smaller than in many socialist countries.[8] To be more precise, these differentials tended to increase up till 1970 and then gradually to decline by a substantial magnitude and to reach levels lower than in 1964. Both in the socialized economy in total and in industry, we observe an increase in interskill differentials after the 1965 reform and a sharp reversal in the postreform period of the 1970s. This decline in skill differentials

Table 2

Skill Differentials in the Whole Socialized Economy of Yugoslavia and in Industry (as a percentage of earnings of the unskilled*)

	1964	1966	1967	1968	1969	1970	1971	1972	1973	1974	1976	1978	1981	1983
						Socialized Economy in Total								
I	268	271	280	274	275	293	280	274	262	269	255	273	261	230
II	205	202	204	198	195	211	208	200	195	197	189	203	198	178
III	176	162	162	159	157	166	161	158	155	161	154	163	160	143
IV	132	126	127	125	123	128	126	122	119	128	121	125	123	111
V	183	188	180	179	180	193	187	187	181	186	176	184	187	168
VI	141	137	132	131	131	138	135	135	135	141	132	140	146	134
VII	112	114	110	110	110	116	112	112	113	116	111	113	121	111
VIII	100	100	100	100	100	100	100	100	100	100	100	100	100	100
(V)	31.4	32.4	34.3	33.4	33.9	35.0	34.4	33.5	32.0	31.5	30.9	32.6	30.1	27.7
Ratio of the highest nonmanual employees to the highest skilled manual workers (category I:V)	146	144	156	153	153	152	150	147	145	145	145	148	140	137

Industry

	1964	1966	1967	1968	1969	1970	1971	1972	1973	1974	1976	1978	1981	1983
I	265	271	262	256	270	299	285	276	257	264	241	259	237	223
II	216	219	217	203	211	225	221	214	199	207	193	209	192	182
III	182	163	160	157	158	170	165	160	154	160	149	157	148	140
IV	140	120	121	117	120	122	118	117	114	123	116	120	114	111
V	190	193	188	181	187	199	196	187	181	184	175	182	174	168
VI	144	135	132	129	130	135	133	132	131	136	126	135	133	131
VII	110	112	110	110	113	115	113	112	110	114	108	111	110	109
VIII	100	100	100	100	100	100	100	100	100	100	100	100	100	100
(V)	31.0	34.0	33.0	32.3	33.8	37.0	36.1	34.8	32.2	32.1	30.4	32.0	29.5	27.4
Ratio of the highest nonmanual employees to the highest skilled manual workers (category I:V)	139.5	140	139	141	144	150	145	148	142	143	138	142	136	133

*Yugoslav statistics distinguish 8 skill categories:

I Employees with full university education
II Employees with 2 years of college or technicum
III Employees with secondary education—gymnasium or technical school—lasting no less than 4 years after primary school
IV Employees with primary general education (8 years)
V Highly skilled manual workers
VI Skilled manual workers
VII Semiskilled manual workers
VIII Unskilled manual workers
Source: Statistical Yearbook of Yugoslavia (SGJ).

was gaining speed in 1981 and 1983.

Dispersion of skill differentials in the republics is in most cases similar to the overall average in Yugoslavia, except in Kosovo (see Appendix, Table B), which consistently outscored all others where inequality of skill differentials is concerned. But here again, no definite and clear relationship exists between the degree of development and dispersion of skill differentials. We find both developed and underdeveloped regions (e.g., Slovenia and Macedonia) with inequalities in skill differentials below the national average. As for changes over time in the dispersion of skill differentials, no discernible trend emerges from our data. With the exceptions of Kosovo, Vojvodina, and Bosnia-Herzegovina, all regions show some decline in dispersion of skill differentials. On balance, the decline seems slightly more pronounced in the two most developed republics, Slovenia and Croatia, than in the less developed republics and provinces.

Data on skill differentials, both for the socialized sector in general and the industrial sector in particular (Table 2), confirm the strong position in the pay scale of highly skilled manual workers, which is in accord with the general tendency in all socialist countries. Highly skilled workers in Yugoslavia on the average earn more than most nonmanual employees. Their average pay is only 10-15% less than the second-highest category of nonmanual workers with two years of college education, and only about 40% less than the highest university-educated personnel. What is even more interesting, this favorable relative position of highly skilled manual workers vis-à-vis nonmanual workers had a tendency to improve over time, except during the period from 1964 to 1969. Moreover, not only have the highly skilled manual workers gained relatively to all categories of nonmanual employees in the period 1964-1983, but, as the data in Table 2 indicate, the unskilled have made even larger relative gains, both in the socialized economy in total and in industry. It is enough to say that whereas in 1964 an unskilled manual worker earned 37.3% of the pay of the highest category of nonmanual employees with university education (see category I in Table 2), in 1983 this ratio had risen to 43.5% (and in industry to 44.8%). Another example of this egalitarian trend is the improved relative position of unskilled manual workers vis-à-vis the lowest category of nonmanual employees (category IV in Table 2). By 1983 unskilled workers' pay was 90% of that of the

Table 3

The Distribution of Enterprises According to Their Spread of Skill Differentials (as a percentage of the total number of enterprises)

The spread of net personal income	1970	1980
1:1.9	29.7	27.5
1:2.9	24.8	29.0
1:3.9	20.2	25.9
1:4.9	12.5	11.7
1:5.9	6.0	3.7
1:6.9	3.1	1.2
1:7.0 and over	4.3	1.0

Source: *Razvoj Jugoslavije*, 1947–1981, p. 159.

lowest nonmanual category (both in the socialized economy in total and in industry), whereas in 1964 this ratio was only 75.72 (in industry, 71.4%).

From the data in Table 2 we can discern that during the reform period of 1965-70, when skill differentials increased, the only beneficiaries were the highly skilled manual workers and the top category of nonmanual workers (category I). The rest, obviously, were losers, and dropped on the income ladder.

Although data on the extreme dispersion of pay between occupations in different enterprises of the socialized sector are not available for every year, such data do exist for some years. They confirm the overall decline of inequality in skill differentials and their relatively low levels. The percentage of enterprises belonging to the socialized sector, with a particular spread of skill differentials, is presented in Table 3.

From Table 3 we can see that enterprises with a spread in skill differentials not higher than 2.9:1 have increased from 54.5% in 1970 to 56.5% in 1980. In the latter year more than 82.4% of firms have a spread not higher than 3.9:1. Thus we observe a sharp decline in the proportion of enterprises having a spread of 4.9:1 and above, from 25.9% in 1970 to 17.6% in 1980. The tendency to reduce skill differentials intensified in the 1980s. In 1983, enterprises with a spread not higher than 2.9:1 and 3.9:1 had reached 60.8% and 85.5%

Table 4

Interbranch Pay Differentials in the Industry in All Yugoslavia and Republics Measured by the Mean and Coefficient of Variation*

Year	In all Yugoslavia		Bosnia-Herzegovina		Montenegro		Croatia		Macedonia	
	x̄	v	x̄	v	x̄	v	x̄	v	x̄	v
1964	380.4	15.5	360.3	19.1	330.4	20.3	389.4	15.6	310.3	17.5
1965	529.3	17.7	498.6	18.6	462.9	20.1	551.3	18.2	418.2	18.5
1966	725.8	18.4	673.4	18.9	627.3	20.4	749.5	18.9	607.4	15.1
1967	817.1	21.3	737.5	19.3	694.5	20.6	840.3	24.5	678.5	20.9
1968	892.2	19.6	882.7	18.4	769.1	19.7	919.3	22.2	746.0	17.9
1969	1,022.3	18.7	940.7	16.7	909.3	21.1	1,064.2	21.8	843.9	20.9
1971	1,461.1	18.0	1,418.3	16.6	1,268.1	20.1	1,588.6	18.9	1,197.3	16.0
1972	1,695.5	15.3	1,605.7	13.9	1,468.7	17.2	1,837.4	16.0	1,401.4	14.1
1973	1,992.6	16.0	1,894.0	13.6	1,708.9	17.7	2,116.2	16.3	1,651.0	13.5
1974	2,566.9	16.3	2,459.2	13.9	2,259.2	17.8	2,691.3	16.2	2,158.1	17.4
1975	3,173.1	16.8	2,986.7	13.7	2,722.4	17.8	3,366.6	15.6	2,666.3	15.0
1976	3,571.7	16.7	3,290.9	15.3	3,083.4	16.6	3,780.5	15.8	2,962.1	16.4
1977	4,164.3	17.1	3,815.8	15.1	3,524.9	18.1	4,340.0	14.5	3,448.1	14.6
1978	4,994.2	17.7	4,577.9	15.2	4,228.9	17.1	5,208.5	17.3	4,211.1	15.3
1979	6,006.9	16.7	5,377.0	14.0	5,101.4	16.0	6,263.0	14.1	5,046.7	15.0
1980	7,359.8	16.5	6,607.4	14.5	6,580.2	15.9	7,761.8	14.0	6,337.7	14.9
1981	10,096.8	14.4	9,127.1	14.0	8,911.7	14.5	10,945.4	15.0	8,592.2	14.4
1982	12,794.9	15.0	11,839.4	14.5	11,451.1	16.2	13,856.4	15.4	11,270.3	14.1
1983	16,370.8	15.3	15,416.3	15.5	13,981.9	20.2	17,584.4	14.9	14,027.6	15.0

Year	Slovenia x̄	v	Serbia x̄	v	Vojvodina x̄	v	Kosovo x̄	v
1964	469.9	16.1	342.2	16.3	336.9	18.3	293.3	19.9
1965	639.0	15.8	479.4	20.0	484.5	22.9	412.3	22.7
1966	839.4	15.0	675.5	21.6	693.1	24.1	578.3	25.6
1967	906.4	15.7	769.6	22.7	762.1	25.6	656.3	25.4
1968	1,022.4	12.9	824.5	21.6	816.2	26.3	717.6	22.5
1969	1,179.5	14.4	949.8	18.3	960.9	25.4	820.3	23.9
1971	1,643.1	11.8	1,330.2	18.4	1,417.9	21.9	1,152.8	21.1
1972	1,942.7	11.1	1,556.9	16.5	1,648.5	20.4	1,342.1	16.6
1973	2,287.9	11.7	1,843.5	18.7	1,900.5	21.4	1,569.3	16.7
1974	2,864.4	13.3	2,447.2	18.7	2,457.6	20.2	2,166.5	18.0
1975	3,522.0	12.9	3,040.5	20.8	3,058.7	20.7	2,607.0	19.1
1976	4,029.7	12.8	3,420.9	21.0	3,471.6	20.9	2,913.9	19.6
1977	4,709.1	10.4	3,978.6	21.6	4,062.1	21.7	3,318.4	17.8
1978	5,702.8	10.1	4,721.6	22.5	4,841.9	21.4	3,914.7	16.8
1979	7,145.8	11.0	5,691.7	22.7	5,785.0	22.2	4,618.8	16.9
1980	8,577.0	12.4	6,972.0	20.8	7,158.7	19.7	5,782.2	15.2
1981	11,292.6	11.6	9,616.6	17.0	9,763.5	15.3	8,360.5	17.0
1982	14,237.6	13.0	12,008.2	17.6	12,382.1	16.5	10,399.1	18.2
1983	18,370.2	12.2	15,492.3	19.0	15,921.5	17.8	12,962.6	19.4

*For the period of 1964–1976 average monthly earnings are recorded in the Yugoslav statistics for 22 industrial branches. In calculating the coefficient of variation for the dispersion of pay between branches, we have excluded the film industry. The figures for this branch are untypical and very erratic through time. After 1976 a more detailed classification was introduced. The amount of industrial branches was increased from 22 to 35 and the film sector has altogether disappeared as a separate branch. In view of the changes in classification of industrial branches after 1976, the coefficient of variation (v) is not fully comparable for the whole period.

respectively.[9] This flattening of skill differentials was a result of faster pay increases for low-skilled workers than for specialists and highly skilled manual workers.

Interbranch Differentials

As can be seen from Table 4, interbranch differentials in industry, measured by the coefficient of variation, are quite large in Yugoslavia, probably larger than in some other socialist countries[10] and larger, according to Estrin, than in most Western countries.[11] But as the data indicate, while inequalities of pay between branches are quite high, they are declining. The increase in interbranch pay differentials after the reform of 1965 was very short-lived; by 1968-69 there was a gradual decline to the levels of 1964. Moreover, in some republics there was no increase at all in interbranch differentials in the reform period of 1965-70, and in some cases (e.g., Slovenia) even a slight decline. A noticeable increase in some years of the reform period took place only in Croatia, Serbia, and Vojvodina. But even where there was an increase in interbranch differentials during this period, it was short-lived, lasting only three or four years, and gave way to a constant decline. This was a result of the postreform pro-egalitarian policy applied by the state in the 1970s.

As for variations in the level of inequality between branches in different republics and autonomous provinces, Slovenia has the lowest level of dispersion of pay between branches and Kosovo has the highest. More importantly, in Slovenia interbranch inequalities of pay, measured by the coefficient of variation, declined rapidly from 1964 to 1983, whereas in Kosovo there have been no discernible changes in this parameter.

With some reservations about the comparability of data for the period under investigation (see the note to Table 4), we may suggest that, unlike the case of interskill differentials, a reasonable correlation exists between the interbranch dispersion of pay and the stage of development of the various regions. With the exception of Vojvodina, the developed regions (Slovenia and Croatia) have lower levels of dispersion of pay than the underdeveloped regions (Bosnia, Montenegro, Macedonia, and Kosovo). The higher dispersion of interbranch differentials in the less developed regions contradicts Estrin's suggestion that regional factors do not add a new dimension to the inequality of pay.[12]

In Yugoslavia the differences in average pay for the same skill, occupation, and job can vary by branch from 1.5 to 2.5 and even more. And it is worth stressing that the interfirm differentials within each branch are also quite large. Although there are no systematic data published about interfirm pay differentials, the sporadic and partial data available convincingly show that these differentials are very substantial. A study done by two Yugoslav economists revealed enormous differences in pay for the same occupation, job, function, or skill in different enterprises in Belgrade. These differences, expressed as a ratio between the maximum and minimum pay for particular functions, are as follows:[13]

Chief director	4.7
Chief of accounting department	4.7
Chief bookkeeper	6.7
Engineer	4.1
Skilled manual worker	3.2
Unskilled worker	3.3
Messenger	3.4
Cleaning woman	3.2

Considering that this large dispersion occurs in a single local labor market in which the supply of labor is relatively abundant as compared with other regions, and in which changing one's workplace in most cases does not require moving to other living quarters, it is safe to infer than on a national scale, differentiation of pay for the same occupation in different enterprises is even larger.[14] The above data also indicate that differences in pay are more pronounced in leading positions than among manual workers.

Extreme differences in pay for the same job in different firms create substantial anomalies in the wage system. A messenger or a cleaning woman can earn more than an engineer, and a highly skilled worker more than a chief director of an enterprise, if the former happens to be employed in an enterprise with very high average pay and the latter in an enterprise with very low average pay. Moving from one enterprise to another can increase one's income by much more than moving up the skill ladder.

Table 5

Average Monthly Net Personal Income per Worker in the Republics and Autonomous Provinces (as a percentage of the national average)

A. *Socialized Economy Total*

	1963	1964	1965	1966	1969	1970	1971	1972	1975	1976	1978	1980	1981	1982	1983
Bosnia-Herzegovina	93	94	96	94	92	95	96	94	95	93	92	91	92	93	95
Montenegro	93	91	89	88	90	89	89	88	88	89	87	90	90	89	84
Croatia	103	104	104	105	106	106	109	110	106	106	107	118	110	110	109
Macedonia	85	86	82	85	85	84	83	84	86	84	83	83	82	83	83
Slovenia	125	130	124	119	116	117	115	116	115	115	116	119	116	115	115
Serbia	92	93	93	96	96	93	94	94	96	96	96	95	95	95	96
Serbia Proper	95	96	96	98	98	95	94	94	95	96	97	96	95	95	95
Vojvodina	89	88	92	95	93	92	96	97	99	100	97	95	98	100	102
Kosovo	79	82	83	85	85	82	82	83	89	86	80	81	83	82	81
Coefficient of variation V (%)	13.7	14.7	13.2	11.2	10.5	11.4	11.2	11.6	9.6	10.3	12.0	14.0	11.8	11.6	12.3
The ratio of the highest to the lowest paid region	158	158	151	140	136	143	140	140	134	137	145	147	141	140	142

B. Industry

Bosnia-Herzegovina	96	99	101	98	96	—	100	98	99	96	93	93	95	96	98
Montenegro	88	90	92	89	93	—	90	89	92	90	89	92	92	92	87
Croatia	102	104	106	106	107	—	112	112	107	106	106	107	109	109	108
Macedonia	83	85	83	86	86	—	86	88	88	86	85	86	85	88	86
Slovenia	125	127	122	117	115	—	113	114	111	113	116	118	113	113	114
Serbia	90	91	91	94	93	—	92	92	95	95	95	95	95	95	95
Serbia Proper	91	92	91	94	94	—	91	91	94	96	96	95	96	95	95
Vojvodina	90	90	91	93	92	—	95	96	98	97	96	96	97	98	99
Kosovo	80	84	88	91	87	—	86	86	90	87	83	85	88	84	85
Coefficient of variation V (%)	14.0	13.7	12.1	9.9	9.7	—	10.5	10.4	8.4	9.0	10.8	10.7	9.3	9.5	10.2
The ratio of the highest to the lowest paid region	156	151	147	136	134	—	131	133	126	131	140	139	133	135	134

Source: Statistical Yearbook of Yugoslavia (SGJ).

Interregional Dispersion

Yugoslavia is a country with vast regional differences in terms of level of development. As a result of these differences, average output per capita and average pay per worker vary a great deal by republic or province. Regional differences in average pay are, however, smaller than the differences in average output per capita. This is a consequence of a deliberate and quite successful state policy applying pressure on the more prosperous enterprises to save a relatively higher proportion of their net output. In general, the proportions allocated to personal income out of net output are therefore lower in the more affluent than in the less affluent regions.

But despite the state's successful efforts to reduce interregional differences in average pay, the disparities are quite substantial. As can be seen from Table 5, dispersion of pay among republics and provinces (measured by the coefficient of variation and the ratio of extremes) had a tendency to decline in the period under investigation. But these disparities in Yugoslavia are still larger than in any other socialist country including the Soviet Union, despite the fact that in the USSR we observe a noticeable increase in interregional disparities of pay.[15]

As for the relative ranking of different republics and provinces in the pay scale, no major change has taken place in the period examined here. Slovenia is permanently the leader, followed by Croatia, while Kosovo and Macedonia continue to lag behind all regions, below Bosnia and Montenegro. The only change that can be observed in the relative ranking of the various regions is in the province of Vojvodina, where average pay during the period under consideration has grown faster than in any other region, establishing it firmly in third place, just above Serbia and Serbia Proper.

Up to this point we have analyzed the dispersion of net personal income almost exclusively within the framework of the socialized sector. This approach is forced upon us by objective difficulties. There are very limited statistical data on an ongoing basis that can be used to analyze dispersions of personal incomes in sectors other than the socialized one. Furthermore, there is an additional, equally important source that contributes to inequality in the distribution of personal incomes, namely, the huge discrepancy between personal incomes in the socialized sector and those in the agricultural sector, which in the Yugoslav context is the only private sector of any importance.[16]

Yugoslavia is in many respects unique as far as differences in earnings between the socialized and the agricultural sectors are concerned. This discrepancy is much larger in Yugoslavia than in most socialist countries (with the possible exceptions of Albania, China, and Romania). The average personal income in (private) agriculture, which still employs over 30% of the labor force, represents no more than 40% of the average personal income in the socialized sector.[17] This ratio was smaller in 1978 than in 1962, suffering its most serious decline between the years 1966 and 1970. In the Soviet Union (which does not have a distinguished record in this field), the ratio of personal incomes in agriculture to those in the socialized sector is about 78%, while Hungary, Poland, and the German Democratic Republic have achieved parity of incomes in the two sectors. It is no exaggeration to state that the private agricultural sector is the pariah, the most neglected and forgotten part of the Yugoslavian economy. According to data provided by some Yugoslav economists,[18] 80% of the village population has incomes below the national average and over 20% lives on the poverty line. This bleak picture is compounded by the fact that a substantial portion of the village population is still without basic social benefits such as pensions, health care, and the like. The village continues to be an important locus of unemployment and a reservoir of cheap, unskilled labor, both for Yugoslavia and for other countries.

Conclusions

To summarize our analysis thus far, we can draw the following conclusions:

(1) The Yugoslav distributional pattern is characterized by low levels of skill differentials and high levels of interbranch and interfirm differentials, which in turn implies that dispersion of pay is substantial within each occupational group and stratum, but very weak between occupational groups and strata. However, despite high interbranch and interfirm differentials, the overall relative dispersion of pay is quite egalitarian, due to the fact that low skill differentials counterbalance the high interbranch and interfirm differentials. The distributional pattern of pay differentials indicates that increases in

inequality of pay among branches and firms do not necessarily increase the stratification of society, if interskill differentials do not increase. This is the case because an increase in interbranch differentials will increase the dispersion of pay within each occupational group and stratum but not between them. The possibility of increasing the relative dispersion of pay without an increase in the stratification of society affords the state an additional element of freedom in its distributional strategy. If the state so desires, it can increase the inequality of pay in the country without creating additional conflicts between strata. However, substantial differences in earnings for the same job, skill, and occupation in different branches and enterprises create political pressures to reduce these differences by administrative measures. Experience has shown that workers in Yugoslavia do not accept substantial differences in pay between enterprises as fair; they demand remuneration more or less equal to that in the most successful enterprises. Thus, great differences in pay for the same job in different branches and enterprises leads to a general rise in earnings in excess of labor productivity.

(2) The Yugoslav system, from the point of view of equality of pay, has not done badly. The general picture of pay inequalities is not worse, and in fact is in many cases even better, than in other socialist countries. The Yugoslav experience suggests that a highly decentralized system of management can have smaller inequalities of pay than a more centralized economy.

(3) From the standpoint of "incentives," however, the Yugoslav system of pay contains the worst possible elements. Employees are reaping high rewards for working in prosperous enterprises to whose success they have contributed very little, because, in most cases, higher incomes are a result of monopolistic practices of all kinds. At the same time, the pay system offers little reward for the contributions employees have actually made; better work and higher skills earn a very small differential. The Yugoslav pay system has not worked out a proper discrimination mechanism against idlers; they get more or less the same pay as the hard-working, and they cannot easily be dismissed unless they commit a serious offense. The inability of the system to deal effectively with these problems increases cynicism and demoralization among workers.

CHAPTER III

Skill Differentials and Self-Management

Let us now turn our attention to those features of the distribution pattern that can be attributed to the economic system itself. We begin with a systematic analysis of interskill differentials. Can we detect a link here between the nature of those differentials and some general systemic features?

Officially there is no labor market in Yugoslavia. Wage labor was abolished with the introduction of self-management, and labor power is no longer considered to be a marketable commodity.[1] The total income of an enterprise belongs to the workers, and they should decide collectively how to divide the net income between personal incomes and other funds. Thus, the argument goes, workers* in the enterprises of the socialized sector do not sell their labor power or working ability at a price established by a contract in the form of collective bargaining or by a state-issued decree. Their pay is not fixed by an agreement made upon their entry into an enterprise. Rather, when a worker becomes a part of the enterprise's labor force, he participates directly—or through a workers' council—in determining the pay differentials of his and other skill categories and, more generally, the principles for the division of the earned income of the enterprise.

What kinds of criteria are used to establish pay differentials? The criteria usually applied are the following: work is more valuable if it is more difficult, dangerous, unpleasant, or complicated, therefore requiring more training and learning. But the decision concerning which work is more valuable depends on the members of the enterprise. It is influenced by supply and demand considerations and by the general prevailing value system of the community at large. In the end, the workers are sovereign in the establishment of these differentials. They make these decisions through a process of negotiation in which different interests must gradually converge and a

---

*In the socialized sector in Yugoslavia, all employees (both manual and non-manual) are called workers. We shall use the same terminology here.

compromise be found. Every member of the work force of the enterprise has a stake in the just distribution of income. As Horvat has said, "Just is what people consider to be just,"[2] and this in turn is influenced by their value system, by ideology. In general in Yugoslavia, the egalitarian ethos has a strong influence, as is evidenced by the fact that skill differentials are smaller than in capitalist countries and have decreased as the country has developed economically. It is notable that various types of manual work considered especially tedious and unpleasant are valued relatively highly.

According to the official creed, since workers themselves determine their wage rates, there should be an incentive to work at full capacity. Hence, Horvat claims that such a distribution is not only just but also optimal. This idealized picture requires some comments. First, it does not address the problem of conflict of interest of various groups and their relative strength. In other words, the problem of power is somehow glossed over. Second, the problem of participation in the process of distribution cannot be separated from the broader issue of effective participation in general in the Yugoslav firm, which is not independent of the power relations in the enterprise and beyond.

Taking the total pool for personal income in a self-managed Yugoslav firm, an increase in pay for one category of employees automatically means a decrease for another. The relative wages of different groups of workers become a zero-sum game. Under these conditions, the collective of workers and its representatives face two contradictory tendencies: the need to differentiate income in accordance with the arduousness, amount, quality, and complexity of work, in order to provide an incentive for good work; and the need to establish reasonable differentials between unskilled and highly skilled workers.

The question to be raised here is, Who represents the first and who the second tendency, and which one ultimately prevails? All the empirical evidence shows that the managers, experts, and skilled manual workers advocate increased material incentives for the sake of efficiency, whereas the less skilled workers press for the leveling of personal incomes. These attitudes are fully in accord with the self-interest of each group. Low-paid workers perceive their income as a residue; if the more highly skilled workers get more, they will get less. The argument that this view is a static one, and that well-paid managers or specialists contribute to a total increase of earnings from which all will benefit, is not always very convincing to those less well paid. The improvement may occur or it may not, and, even if it does, it will be some time in the future. For low-paid workers, money today is much more valuable than money tomorrow.

Although the groups representing both of these tendencies have some influence in the democratic process of decision making,[3] their relative strength is far from equal. Such a "political" mechanism for establishing skill differentials is bound to create fluctuations both in time and in space. Due to differences, as well as changes, in the balance of forces in different enterprises, interskill differentials vary considerably by enterprise and have a tendency to fluctuate over time.

It is claimed by many advocates of participatory industrial democracy that, in an environment where workers identify themselves with the firm due to their direct participation in decision making, smaller skill differentials will not diminish work effort, responsibility, and the desire for advancement in one's career. There is considerably less reliance upon personal incentives in a participatory work environment.

The adherents of industrial democracy (like the traditional left in general) question the effectiveness of wage differentials and close supervision for motivating worker effort. According to some scholars in this field, especially industrial psychologists and sociologists,[4] work effort has three dimensions: duration, intensity, and quality. The worker has ultimate control over the second and third of these. But material incentives and organizational controls are external to the worker, and in practice even elaborate external incentives can fail to stimulate top productive performance. A participatory work environment, according to such writers as Vanek, Espinosa, and Zimbalist, enhances the probability that the worker will internalize the goals of the enterprise. Once the process of goal internalization begins, sources of effort untapped by external incentives are progressively opened and the potential comes closer to being realized.[5]

A similar view is expressed by Williamson. He argues that market relations presume and legitimize a calculating mentality. Unless this is offset by some form of social control, *quid pro quo* relations (payment for effort) invite individualistic, free-riding exploitation of flaws in the management system.[6] Even capitalist firms, argues Williamson, introduce certain forms of social control to induce social obligation and in this way to modify the calculating mentality. Other examples of social control cited by many authors include mores encouraging hard work and respect and adherence to authority. The seniority system is yet another device to create a long-term relationship and sense of obligation between workers and firms. Successful social control instruments, according to Carter, "create an expectation of long-run fair and reciprocal obligation, and lessen the need for precise short-run accounting of individual behavior."[7]

Although most participatory enterprises do still maintain skill differentials (since goal internalization is a long and gradual process), inequality of remuneration and reliance upon personal incentives are significantly reduced in a self-managed environment, according to the proponents of industrial democracy. The examples of Maoist China, the Yugoslav firms, enterprises in Chile during the Allende government, and the Mondragon cooperatives (where skill differentials are much smaller than in the rest of Spanish industry) are used to argue that worker-created structures are more equal than those imposed by the capitalist system; and further, that equalization of wages does not reduce motivation, because it creates worker solidarity, whereas very large differentials divide the work force and foster internal rivalries.

The evidence that self-managed enterprises in general, and those in Yugoslavia in particular, have smaller differentials than capitalist firms is very strong. But can we link this with the specific nature of self-management in Yugoslavia? A cautionary note is in order here. Although formally, social control devices are probably easier to introduce under self-management, whether or not they are successful depends to a large degree on the genuineness of participation in general, and particularly where issues of personal income distribution are concerned. A sea of ink has been used to describe how very often self-management in Yugoslavia has degenerated into a mere formality, whereby the collective rubber stamps the decision of the power elite, usually composed of the top management and the trade union and party bosses.

All the evidence from sociological research indicates that the majority of semi-skilled and unskilled manual workers in Yugoslav industry do not participate in the activity of the workers' councils, and that they behave as traditional wage laborers. Considering that these two skill groups represent the majority of manual workers, and that they account for 70-80% of workers' council membership, the scope of participation is sharply reduced. Indeed, even the participation of skilled workers in the decision-making process of the firm is far from impressive. A survey conducted by Obradović for twenty industrial enterprises in four republics over a period of three years indicates that the managerial staff plays a decisive role in the decision-making process, especially when technical, organizational, or market-oriented issues are discussed.[8] According to this survey, members of the executive group take up 80% of the total time spent in the discussions of the workers' council; they provide 70% of all explanations; and 75% of all proposals that are accepted were offered by members of this group. What is more, the above-cited study and other surveys also report a very high correlation between the hierarchical status of the individual in the firm and his level of participation in the workers' council; the higher one's position on the executive ladder, the more intensive is his participation.

It is to be expected that managers would play a major role in decisions about technical matters, marketing, and cooperation inside and outside the firm, since these require competence and expertise. But, surprisingly, even in matters of income distribution and working conditions, where we would expect the most intensive worker participation in decision-making, the situation is not what one might predict. Seventy percent of all employees (mostly the unskilled and semi-skilled), according to Obradović's study, participate very little or not at all in discussions about income distribution and related matters. It is enough to say that of all the proposals accepted in this area, 86% were made by managers, who comprise no more than 8% of the total work force.[9]

Although it is not our aim to give a full analysis of the reasons why the real status of the workers in decisionmaking is so weak, a brief description of a few points of view is very suggestive.

(1) Social power, according to the distinguished Yugoslav sociologist J. Županov,[10] is distributed hierarchically in favor of the leading personnel, with workers having the least power. From this point of view, the situation is not essentially different from the existing industrial organization in the West. The reason why social power has not changed in the Yugoslav firm is linked with the fact that, as hierarchical organization has survived, so has hierarchical

subordination. The key position of management in the communication process and in coordination has not been affected by the introduction of the formal structure of self-management. Management has retained the strategic position in dealing with external demands and environmental pressures stemming from technological and market forces. Although formally managers are not granted entrepreneurial prerogatives (this authority belongs to the workers' council), in reality they are better equipped to carry out these functions. Županov's conclusions in this matter are worth quoting:

> . . . Even the most radical changes in the formal institutional blueprint do not assure an effective participation of employees, for they do not necessarily redress the power imbalance between management and employees which is inherent in industrial organizations everywhere. In other words, they do not overcome the power barrier to successful participation.[11]

(2) The existing model of self-management organization is composed of two different structures which are not quite compatible: a hierarchical one functioning in the daily work process, and a non-hierarchical one functioning only sometimes. But each of these structures is based on a different definition of the producer's role, and on different organizational principles.

(3) Self-managed firms cannot be fully autonomous in a market environment. Inside the enterprise the workers are formally autonomous and equal, but in the market situation they are dependent and unequal. The fact that factors outside the control of the workers' council (the possibility of financing investment from credit, the market price, the demand for goods on the market, prices of inputs, etc.) become more important for the success of the firm than the workers' own efforts, reduces worker interest in what is going on in the enterprise. As a result, the issues that are discussed and decided on in the workers' council are secondary. This means that genuine self-management in a single unit is not really possible. Only in a broader framework can it make sense, namely if workers are able to control the surplus on a national scale via a vertically integrated central workers' council.[12]

(4) Even under the best of circumstances, full-scale council

democracy, where decisions are taken by general vote, can work efficiently only in rather small groups, because there is a limit to the capacity to process information. As Williamson points out, "Everything cannot be communicated to everyone and joint decisions reached without preempting valuable time that could be productively used for other purposes. Since the number of linkages in all channel networks goes up as the square of the number of members, peer group size is perforce restricted."[13] It is possible that this informational constraint is not as strong as Williamson describes, but there is no question that the larger the size of the collective, and the less transparent and simple the information structure, the more difficult it is to make decisions on a broad democratic basis. The attempt in Yugoslavia in the 1970s to break up two big firms into small units of associated labor (BOALS) was intended to make self-management more meaningful; but this, as we know, comes into collision with the technical requirements of coordination and planning. The dismemberment of firms into small units, and the introduction of market exchange between the associated labor units in the larger firm, proved costly and inefficient, especially where economies of scale play an important role. A retreat from this fragmentation is under way. New proposals suggest that the independence of BOALS should be limited, and especially that commercial trading between them should cease.[14]

Whatever the reasons for the weak status of workers in enterprise decision making, the relatively small skill differentials in the Yugoslav economy can be linked with its self-management only if we assume that the majority of employees participate effectively in the decisions on distribution of personal income. If, however, this is not the case, we must look for other explanations. We would suggest that egalitarian socialist ideology has played an important role in establishing low skill differentials, independently of the self-management system.

Studies done by some Yugoslav economists and sociologists[15] indicate that egalitarianism is the dominant value shared by those employed in industry. For workers, equality and equity rank highest of all values, while self-management and solidarity rank very low among both workers and managers. But managers, by contrast with workers, give very little value to equality, stressing instead personal freedom, payment according to work, etc., which of course is not unexpected for this social stratum.

In view of the overwhelming superiority of management (especially top management) in the enterprise decision-making process, including decisions about income distribution, the question arises as to how the egalitarian ethos of the majority of workers is translated into egalitarian skill differentials, despite management opposition.

Obradović's survey indicated that members of the League of Communists participate very actively in the decision-making process of the workers' council on all subjects, and especially intensively on matters of personal income distribution. This is not surprising, considering that the majority of executives and many experts are party members.

Although on most issues the League of Communists, especially its secretary in the firm, sides with the top management (there being a strong connection between the political and technological structures in the enterprise) in matters of income distribution and relations with the outside world, the party elite's view differs in many instances from that of the managerial elite. The party sides with the values of the majority of workers and exerts influence on the managers and trade unions in support of an egalitarian pay structure. These matters are thus determined more by political aims and motives than by economic ones. The influence of the League of Communists on the income distribution in the enterprise is therefore a sort of "indirect" state intervention.

The egalitarian tendency to level off skill differentials was reinforced by the economic crisis in the 1980s, when real personal income declined substantially. By the end of the 1970s, some republics (notably Serbia) had established guidelines[16] for average skill differentials in order to protect low paid groups from economic crisis and falling real incomes; but these were soon abolished because the actual dispersion of skill differentials was even lower than the prescribed guidelines. A decline of the total sum available for distribution in the enterprises[17] has forced a compromise in favor of the lower and average paid workers.[18] It is difficult not to agree here with Bićanić when he claims that the economic crisis in Yugoslavia has made the problem of distribution more acute and has strengthened egalitarian tendencies—as he calls it, the perception of equal stomachs.[19]

To conclude this part of our analysis, the egalitarian tendency is not specific to the Yugoslav self-management system. It was, after all, well pronounced before self-management was fully established. What is more, egalitarian skill differentials were and are in evidence in other socialist countries.

CHAPTER IV

Interbranch Pay Differentials and Self-Management

We shall now investigate the link between interbranch and interfirm pay differentials and the Yugoslav economic system. The point of departure for our analysis will be an overview and critique of different theories as to why interbranch and interfirm differentials in Yugoslavia are as large as they are, a question that has been widely debated in economic literature, both in the West and in Eastern Europe. We can distinguish three main schools of thought about the nature of income distribution in Yugoslavia: the labor school, the capital school,[1] and the property rights school. Following a brief description of each, we shall offer a critical appraisal.

The Labor School

The labor school of wage determination applies the neoclassical static equilibrium analysis of capitalism to the Yugoslav firm, to show that specific differentials are created in the framework of self-management.[2] Adherents of this school claim that the differences in wages in different enterprises and branches are linked with the logic of self-management, and that they are too large to be explained by economic policy alone. This school of thought, like the others under review, assumes that a firm under labor management will maximize income per worker,[3] in contradistinction to the capitalist firm, where the objective function is the size of profit.

The labor school also assumes that there is no labor market under Yugoslav self-management, hence labor mobility is restricted. As a result, differences in the marginal product of labor will not be equalized, and certain firms will have permanent gains which will not be transferred to other enterprises.

According to Estrin, a prominent figure in the labor school, in a capitalist economy, an increase or decrease of marginal product leads to the hiring or firing of workers, so that labor is attracted from firms with low, and to firms with higher, values of marginal product. This process of reallocation continues until efficiency is restored in the labor market. But in a self-managed firm, Estrin argues, an increase in the price of its products automatically leads to increased earnings, since a lack of labor mobility prevents entry into high-earning enterprises. As a result, wages and marginal products of labor are not equalized in different uses, and the more "successful" firms permanently enjoy higher wages.

Because a lack of labor mobility prevents an efficient allocation of labor, Pareto's optimum cannot be achieved. Assuming a suboptimal allocation of labor, it follows that, if a proper reallocation of labor between firms were to take place, the level of output could be increased. Furthermore, a more efficient allocation of labor would reduce interfirm differentials. On this point in particular, Ward was probably the first in the labor school to use neoclassical tools to argue that interfirm differences in income in Yugoslavia are a result of an inefficient allocation of labor.

The fact that labor is not mobile and is inefficiently allocated points to the conclusion that under self-management firms employ less labor than they would under more developed labor market conditions. The gist of the argument is as follows: Given that the objective function of the self-management firm is the maximization of income per worker, the marginal product of labor must be equal not to the wage rate (w), as in a capitalist firm, but to income per worker (y). Assuming the law of diminishing returns, it follows then that workers' income in a socialist firm must be larger than capitalist wages ($y > w$) in an identical capitalist firm where profit is positive. A self-managed firm will therefore employ fewer workers and use a more capital-intensive method than its capitalist counterpart. Hence the model predicts high rates of unemployment and a labor-saving tendency under self-management.

A variety of points have been made, on both the theoretical and the empirical plane, to prove that the neoclassical static equilibrium concept is inappropriate for analysis of the Yugoslav firm. In particular, the theory's predictions about the behavior of the Yugoslav self-managed firm with respect to employment and dispersion of incomes are seriously questioned by many authors,[4] and most notably by Branko Horvat.[5]

Horvat rejects the explanation of the neoclassical school in general, and the labor school in particular, as to the reasons for the large interbranch differentials in Yugoslavia. According to Horvat, free entry is more easily achieved in the framework of social property than under private property; hence, there are no systemic obstacles to the equalization of income per worker throughout the economy, especially in conjunction with the imposition of a uniform price for the use of capital, in which case both distributed wages and undistributed profits could be equalized among firms and branches.

Horvat believes that there is a tendency in Yugoslavia to equalize wages among firms and branches, notwithstanding the differences in income per worker. Because the principle of distribution according to work is so strongly entrenched in the self-managed economy, enterprises with higher-than-average incomes per worker will tend to save a higher proportion of their net income than enterprises with below-average performance. But this permits the more efficient enterprises to accumulate a larger part of their income. Horvat admits that, in the end, the more dynamic and innovative enterprises will have both higher wages and profit. He partially accepts that the self-managed system, if left alone, would produce wage differentials due to differences in economic performance; this is why state intervention is required to equalize wages, implementing the principal of distribution according to work. Unfortunately, the state is not doing its job in this field, which explains the existence of unwarranted differentials. But it is striking that Horvat does not explain why the state is not doing its job, and why this "neglect" has persisted for so long. Reading Horvat, one is left with a strong impression that the implemented state policies are just a reflection of the lack of expertise and competence of the planners and officials. No doubt these factors are of some importance in the Yugoslav socioeconomic environment, but, as we will attempt to argue later on, they do not add up to an explanation of the phenomena that concern us here.

The Capital School

The capital school, represented by Vanek, Jovićić, Milenkovitch, and Staellers,[6] links the differences in incomes and high capital-labor ratios in Yugoslavia not with the imperfections of the labor market or with the specific property rights of the Yugoslav firm, but rather with the imperfections of the capital market. According to this intellectual tradition, maldistribution of income, which is a signal that the Pareto optimum has not been reached, is strictly linked with inefficient allocation of resources.

Within the framework of the capital school, inefficiencies in income distribution are explained by the low price of capital, resulting in its rationing, which allows enterprises with privileged access to credit to acquire a quasi rent which is distributed to workers as wages. A lack of capital mobility prevents equalization of price for that factor of production and does not allow the efficient allocation of assets; this in turn produces a quasi rent which is the difference between the marginal product and the cost of capital. Workers appropriate this difference from the capital allocated to their firm by the planners. Better access to capital, in one form or another, creates this kind of monopoly quasi rent, and is mostly manifested in firms and branches with high capital-labor ratios (K/L).[7] The greater the share of capital in the formation of net output, the greater the possibility of earning such a quasi rent. If enterprises were to be charged a price on capital reflecting scarcity (a price equal to the marginal productivity of capital), the quasi rent would disappear, and the extra differentiation of wages among firms and branches for the same skill profession would disappear along with it. A low cost of capital (below the marginal productivity) not only creates unequal distribution of incomes, due to variation of rent in different industries, but is bound to produce unnaturally high capital-labor ratios and, consequently, small potential to increase employment in the firms.

According to Vanek, this tendency for excessive capital intensity is exacerbated by some specific state policies intended to prevent excessive income inequalities. The social agreements requiring that branches and firms with higher-than-average incomes should save a higher percentage than those with lower-than-average incomes are, even if well intended, counterproductive. The end result of such intervention is a further increase in the capital intensity of the economy. This is so because, in a situation where there is no control over the particular capital intensities, firms with larger savings will install more labor-saving equipment, which will further increase labor productivity and incomes, setting the stage for further capital-intensive accumulation. This cumulative process is succinctly described by Vanek: "rich enterprises will grow richer, the poor ones and the unemployed will be left behind."[8] (A similar point is made by Popov, another proponent of the capital school in Yugoslavia.)

Vanek sees the process of self-financing of investment as one of the major stumbling blocks hindering the remedy of the shortcomings of the Yugoslav economy in general, and the maldistribution of wages in particular.[9] Under a usufructus property regime, self-financing prevents the equalization of marginal productivities of capital in different uses, because the time preferences of working collectives vary significantly. He advocates a switch from internal to external funding, to a pure rental process of investment which, together with a proper price for capital and more developed capital markets, would permit an efficient allocation of capital under the existing property relations. Vanek makes the following points in defense of external funding.

First, he claims that external funding is philosophically and ideologically more in tune with the property relations in Yugo-slavia—with the usufructus regime—simply because the capital stock cannot be traced to those individuals who have created it. In reality all Yugoslavs have created this capital; therefore the interest and rents from such capital should belong to society as a whole. In Yugoslavia, however, workers earn and consume rent on alienated labor other than their own, and at the same time they collectively save funds which they cannot recuperate. Economic power in Yugoslavia, Vanek complains, depends, to a degree, on the amount of capital that organizations have at their disposal, and not only on their labor potential. He assesses self-financing of investment as an aberration in the labor-managed economy, something that is inconsistent with its very nature and should be abolished.

Second, Vanek argues that under a usufructus regime, the return on investment must be very high before the working collective will want to invest from its own resources. This is so because individual workers can expect returns from the new investment only in the form of increased future incomes; they cannot recover the principal. Nor do they have a claim on the assets generated; for the new assets are an addition to collective property over which individual workers have no right to dispose. To make collective saving attractive, it must bring higher returns than individual saving (in a bank), in order to recompense the loss of principal. Moreover, the difference between bank interest on savings and the rate of return on self-financed investment that is required to make such investment an attractive alternative will vary with people's expected years of employment, and thus with the average age of a collective.

The confusion and inefficiency this brings to the allocation of scarce capital resources is obvious. Different collectives will have different time preferences as to the distribution of net income, and therefore marginal productivities of capital will not be equalized. Hence capital will not be efficiently allocated. Another result will be different wages for the same job in different branches and enterprises. This can be remedied if external funding is introduced and a real scarcity price is charged for capital. Here it should be noted that the difficulties of saving collectively in the framework of the property regime of Yugoslavia, emphasized by Vanek, are very similar to those emphasized by the Furubotn-Pejović property rights school. However, Vanek draws completely different conclusions from this shortcoming. He argues that the problem can be cured simply by abolishing self-financing, and without changing the property relations. As we will see below, the property rights school is much less optimistic in this regard.

Third, Vanek makes the point that self-financing under Yugoslav property relations creates antagonism between the oldtimers, some of whom are the founders of the firm, and the newcomers. The former may always feel that they have contributed most to the firm, certainly much more than recent entrants. Naturally this leads to a situation of first- and second-class citizenship within the firm. This negative phenomenon would disappear if funding were external, making work the only common element, linking oldtimers and newcomers.

Fourth, the basis of a cooperative worker-managed firm should be the work in common, and not ownership in common, or a combination of work and ownership in common. To avoid alienation in the Marxian sense, participatory firms must be based entirely on participation in work. Mixing participation in work and participation by ownership injects the poison of alienation into the self-managed firm. What is more, external financing of capital puts capital on the same footing as all other nonhuman factors of production, whereas self-financing on the level of the firm gives capital the same or higher status than labor.

Finally, Vanek argues that in a socialist society the investment process is a common venture for the enterprise and society at large, both in terms of benefits to be derived and responsibilities to be assumed. Investment projects should therefore be scrutinized and judged not only by the firm, but also by society represented by some institution (Vanek suggests a National Labor Management Agency, or some lending institution). Under self-financing a firm does not need to consult anyone or conform with any national development plan, which can create serious inefficiencies, due to a lack of broader information (e.g., externalities). Considering that the investment process involves both the firm and society, the risk of possible failure should also be shared. Under external financing, when an investment fails both parties share the cost of the loss of the value of the invested assets. Under self-financing, however, only the collective of the firm pays the price for failure, despite the fact that the success or failure of an investment depends not only on the firm, but also on the actions taken by society as a whole.[10]

Vanek also rejects the labor school's explanation of the differentials for the same job in various branches in Yugoslavia. His views on this matter demand our attention. Vanek admits that efficient allocation of capital does not automatically guarantee an efficient allocation of labor or an equalization of incomes for the same job, occupation, or profession in different industries and firms; but he believes that this is easier to achieve in Yugoslavia than equalization of the marginal product of capital.

According to Vanek there are three reasons why labor incomes in enterprises and branches can differ:

(1) Some firms may operate on a less efficient scale in the same branch. This deficiency can be overcome by bringing the firm to an efficient scale of operation.

(2) Incomes are different in different branches and firms (even after paying the full price for capital), due to different demand and price conditions; some firms can charge relatively high prices because demand is high. But these monopolistic tendencies are weak in Yugoslavia because, according to Vanek, there are strong stimuli to enter industries with high incomes. The state, by stimulating entry of

new firms or by encouraging expansion of existing ones, satisfies the strong demand and thus reduces prices in high-income branches. In this manner the state helps to overcome monopolistic tendencies.

(3) Differences in productivity in the same branch, due to differences in technology, other than those linked with X-efficiency, will always exist. These differences can, however, be reduced by a spread of information and dissemination of the most advanced technology. Vanek is convinced that differences in income resulting from the above-mentioned causes can be overcome, as long as entry between branches is assured or expansion of the existing branches takes place. This is why he stresses the price of capital, rather than the price of labor, as the main source of income inequalities.

A few comments are appropriate here concerning Vanek's ideas about the "evil" of self-financing and the virtue of external financing of investment. Many economists, both in the West and in Yugoslavia, question Vanek's assertion that self-financing is at the root of investment inefficiencies, creates a disincentive to save collectively, and accounts for differences in earnings for similar jobs. External financing is not, they maintain, the panacea for these shortcomings. The gist of their arguments can be captured in the following points:

(1) The advocates of external financing of investment do not take into consideration the hazard connected with debt financing. Limited liability allows borrowers to get rid of a part of their obligation by dissolving the enterprise. External finance will make the option of bankruptcy more attractive. When this happens, the cost to creditors increases. The credit system, defensively anticipating this possibility, will include the risk of default in the price of lending money. A pure rental economy with exclusively external financing is therefore no solution. What is suggested instead is a rather moderate change of the property regime, giving the workers a claim not only to incomes but, at least partially, to assets as well, along the lines of the Mondragon solution.[11]

(2) Vanek's claims that external financing is always optimal is exaggerated. Under certain circumstances self-financing can be a cheaper source of finance for investments. But, according to Bonin, the specific form of investment is not the source of inefficiency in the accumulation process;[12] the cause of inefficiency is the existing property regime in Yugoslavia, which does not stimulate a proper care

of capital assets by the workers.

(3) In the Yugoslav environment very few economists advocate a pure rental economy along the lines proposed by Vanek; but the merits and demerits of internal and external financing are discussed widely.[13] The adherents of self-financing argue that this form of financing investment gives workers better control over the process of expanded reproduction and enhances the self-managing role of the working collective. But this position does not go unopposed. There are those who argue that credit financing is more desirable than internal financing from the workers' point of view. This line of reasoning points to the fact that workers usually prefer short-term investment over long-term investment. The reason for this is that the former yields quick returns and ensures improvements in working conditions, while the latter may very well create labor-saving conditions, which raises fears of unemployment, no matter how profitable the investment may be in the long run. Managers, on the other hand, tend to prefer long-term investment, irrespective of the location of the firm and irrespective of the immediate benefits it may bring to the self-managed community. Thus it is necessary that some sort of compromise be reached with the short-term investment interest of the workers; and this, of course, presupposes a compromise between external borrowing and self-financing.

Another argument advanced by those who defend the superiority of borrowed funds is that the commercial banks, formally independent of the state since the 1960s, lend money (at least in theory) only on the basis of strict criteria of profitability. Enterprises that borrow money are obliged to utilize it only for the completion of a specific project, under strict supervision. It is assumed that the bank has greater expertise and judgment than the enterprise in the efficient allocation of investment. Be that as it may, the experience of the last ten to fifteen years has shown that, irrespective of the source of investment financing, there have been many projects undertaken that were misconceived and should not have been begun in the first place. This failing, as far as external funding is concerned, is linked with the fact that the criteria for borrowing funds are not always based on economic calculations, but rather on political patronage and influence and the lobbying efforts of powerful enterprises. As a result of these malpractices there is now a serious liquidity problem.[14] Many firms have been unable to pay back the funds they borrowed and, worse, most of them get away with it. Ultimately, the consequences of failure for a Yugoslav firm are not very different from those for a Soviet-type enterprise whose risk is socialized, with the treasury covering the losses. This having been said, all the available data point indisputably to a low and declining efficiency of investment in the socialized economy in Yugoslavia, irrespective of the sources of investment financing.[15]

Finally, it should be noted that the so-called capital price school, whose major proponents are Bajt, Horvat, Mihailović, and Popov,[16] represent a variant of the Western capital school. They attribute inefficiencies in the allocation of resources to capital shortages, inefficient rationing procedures for capital, and low or negative interest rates. The capital price school is popular in Yugoslavia, probably because it does not link shortcomings in the allocation of resources with the very core of the system, that is, with self-management *per se*.

The Property Rights School

The third stream—the property rights school—holds that one of the characteristics of property relations in Yugoslavia is a lack of individual property rights, which in turn works as a hindrance to the mobility of both labor and capital. A worker in a Yugoslav enterprise, unlike some other forms of cooperative (e.g., Mondragon),[17] cannot take away the proportion of funds which he has accumulated as part of the enterprise's capital stock when he leaves his job. He enjoys the benefits of investment funds in the form of a larger personal income, better working conditions, and so forth, but only as long as he stays with the firm. The same is true regarding workers' investment in collective consumption services. They enjoy the benefits of kindergartens, hospitals, cafeterias, housing, etc., only as long as they are with the firm.

The longer a worker stays with the firm, the larger is the return on his investment; the larger is the proportion of nonpecuniary benefits in the total income, and therefore the stronger is his determination to stay with the firm. Those who remain in the firm and those who join it, even if they make very little contribution to the investment fund, take over the benefits of those who invested their income in the enterprise for a prolonged period.[18] For all these reasons, workers are not inclined to change jobs and lose their benefits.

Since workers' income and nonpecuniary benefits depend not only on their own effort, but also on how much capital was accumulated in previous years, moving to another enterprise may bring a reduction in one's personal income and benefits if the new enterprise has accumulated less capital than the previous one.[19] Under these circumstances, the likelihood of a worker switching from one enterprise to another would be greatly enhanced if some compensation for the loss of his investment in nonowned assets were to be awarded to him. This compensation would go beyond just higher pay; the worker would also be able to consider to what extent the proposed employment promised a superior income stream over his planned employment period.

For comparative purposes it should be emphasized here that the property rights school, like those we have already discussed, does not deny that low mobility of labor and capital is the reason why the pay for the same job varies in different branches and enterprises. But, in contradistinction to the others, it identifies as the most important cause of that low mobility, and the consequent interbranch differentials, the specific property regime in Yugoslavia, rather than the maximand of Yugoslav firms (as argued by the labor school) or specific imperfections of the capital markets—self-financing and the wrong price of capital (as the capital school claims).

Having said that, however, we should stress that like the others, the property rights school, especially as represented by the Furubotn-Pejović version, is well embedded in the neoclassical tradition. All of them link the inability to equalize marginal productivities of labor and capital, and hence to achieve Pareto optimum, with the imperfections of the market. They differ when it comes to explanations. The property rights school blames these problems mainly on the lack of individual property rights in Yugoslavia, whereas for the others this is only one of the factors, and not the most important one, explaining interbranch differentials.

According to the property rights school, the lack of individual property rights, which deprives the worker of the possibility to take away his or her reinvested funds when he leaves the firm, not only creates specific interbranch differentials, but also substantially reduces the incentive to save in a Yugoslav firm. Under these circumstances it only stands to reason that younger members are usually more inclined to reinvest than either their older colleagues nearing the age of retirement or those who do not want to stay in the firm for a long time. This situation is reinforced by the fact that pensions in Yugoslavia are linked to the size of personal income in the last five years before retirement and do not reflect the income generated by the worker over the years, including his contribution to the reinvestment fund.

It is worth examining further how the property rights school explains the roots of the Yugoslav firm's low propensity to save. The version that has received the most attention in Western academic circles was developed by Pejović and Furubotn in a series of articles.[20] They propose that the decline in the propensity to save in a firm should be explained by the peculiar nature of the relationship of the collective to the net worth of the firm. The gist of the argument is that the firm's collective has two options for the income they do not wish to consume: they can either allocate it to the personal income fund and then put it into a bank time deposit, or they can turn it back to the firm for investment in income-earning assets.[21] Once the income is reinvested in the firm, it cannot be reappropriated. Only the fruit ("usufructus")[22] in the form of net income will be available to them, and that only for as long as they stay with the firm. In other words, the workers lose all rights to the principal sum that they plough back into the firm; in Western terms, the collective makes a sort of investment in an annuity for a fixed number of years, with no recovery of capital. In contrast to reinvestment, savings out of personal income not only yield continuous income, but the principal sum belongs to the worker. This is why, in order for these two alternative investments to become equally attractive to workers' collectives, the rate of return on nonowned assets must not be just marginally larger than the interest paid on private saving deposits, but larger by a sufficient magnitude to compensate for the loss of principal.

More precisely, it has been argued that the critical rate of return (r^*) which makes investment in nonowned assets and in private assets equally attractive, depends on the planned time horizon of the collective (measured by the average expectation of the collective to stay employed in the firm); on the actual rate of return on capital in the firm; and on the level of interest paid for private savings deposits (So). It follows then that the shorter the planned time horizon of the collective, and/or the higher the (So), and/or the lower the marginal productivity of capital in the firm, the less attractive nonowned assets become in comparison with owned assets. In Yugoslavia, according to the property rights school, the planning time horizon is never long enough to make the return on nonowned assets as attractive as owned assets. If the time horizon is not very long, ($r*$) will be substantially larger than returns on owned private assets unless the rate of return on nonowned assets is very high.[23] Given the interest rate for private savings and the actual rate of return in Yugoslavia, it would require a 17-20 year time horizon for the collective to make these two alternative allocations equally attractive.[24] According to Furubotn-Pejović, the planned time horizon of the typical Yugoslav firm is much shorter than this requirement; hence there is no incentive for the workers to divert funds from their net income to self-financed investment.

The incentive for self-financing is also weakened by the fact that the bank rate is lower than the critical rate of return. Therefore, even when investment in nonowned and owned assets is equally attractive, workers' collectives will prefer to borrow funds, if available, as long as their expected return on investment is larger than the interest paid to the bank for the loan.

The property rights school of Furubotn-Pejović does not deny that credit in a growth-oriented system can formally replace self-financing, in order to achieve national development objectives. But this will be conducive to a consumption bias and an overall decline in the propensity to save. Under the Yugoslav property regime, credit cannot entirely replace self-financing because there is an inverse relationship between external and internal financing of investment. With an increase in external funding, a decrease in internal funding of investment takes place. More and more funds are directed to wages. What is more, the propensity to save out of wages declines, and we observe a general retardation of voluntary savings and a higher propensity to consume. This is so because under the Yugoslav property regime, workers tend to perceive that high wages and high levels of consumption are compatible with high rates of capital expansion of the firm as long as there is an elastic credit system. The net result is an investment rate larger than the full-employment level of saving, accompanied by strong inflationary pressures.

The implication of this analysis is that self-managed firms under the Yugoslav property regime will avoid self-financed investment. Given the fact that bank credit is not an alternative to the lack of propensity to save by the firm, Furubotn and Pejović predict stagnation and strong inflationary pressures. They therefore assert that no remedy is possible for the shortcomings of the accumulation process in Yugoslavia, short of granting workers' collectives full property rights over capital assets (equity capital).

Adherents of the more moderate wing of the property rights school do not share this point of view.[25] In fact they support Vanek's idea that outside financing can, to some degree, solve the problem of investment of the self-managed economy. Hence, a collective's lack of interest in saving their own funds would not lead to a lack of interest in outside funds for investment; outside financing allows future consumption of the workers to increase without reducing current consumption. What is more, outside financing mitigates the conflict between the oldtimers and the newcomers, since the newly employed not only participate in the fruit of investment, they also share in the burden of paying off the borrowed investment funds.

It should be noted that there is another branch of the property rights school which draws a completely opposite conclusion from the Furubotn-Pejović argument about the propensity to invest in non-owned assets. The Polish property rights school explains the high propensity to appropriate the surplus as a substitute for property rights.[26] The high propensity to invest via heavy borrowing is, according to them, a specific form of surplus appropriation in view of the inability to do it in any other way.

Let us now turn our attention to a critical assessment of the property rights school. First and foremost, Yugoslav reality does not verify the stagnation theory of the radical segment of the property rights school. Apart from the 1980s, when there has been a stagnation of the rate of growth,[27] we observe in Yugoslav firms a rather strong accumulation drive throughout the postwar era. Indeed, overinvestment rather than underinvestment was the norm. In spite of some relative erosion of enterprise self-financed investment in favor of external financing over the long run, the saving ratios out of the firm's net income have been high by any standard.

It must be stressed here that the very high rate of saving in the Yugoslav firm in the postwar period does not itself disprove the Furubotn-Pejović prediction that savings in the Yugoslav firm will dry out. This stream of the property rights school analyzes the internal logic of the firm, assuming an autonomous working collective which has the right independently to decide how to divide its net income between wages and savings. But such full autonomy was never granted to the enterprises as far as accumulation is concerned. The state, one way or another, has intervened in order to guarantee a certain level of internal saving in the socialized firms. For this purpose the state has used a few major economic policy tools in various periods with different degrees of force. First, with the exception of the period between 1965 and 1972, every republic has had a parameter of distribution regulating the ratio of personal income to other funds. Enterprises with higher earned net incomes than the average must save a higher proportion of their incomes than enterprises with lower net incomes. This intervention in the distributional pattern tries to achieve two objectives: (a) to assure self-financed investment, and (b) to reduce differences in personal incomes in different enterprises and branches (so that the differences among enterprises in terms of personal income will be smaller than differences in net income). Second, the amount of credit a firm can get for investment has always been linked in some way with the magnitude of its own savings.

These regulations, enforced by the state, were only partially successful in guaranteeing high rates of self-financed investment. After 1965, when the state gave enterprises more discretion over income distribution, saving rates fell and a larger proportion of investment was financed through bank credit.[28] But what is striking even during that period is the fact that internal savings fell to the much lower but still respectable rate of 15-21% of the net income in the socialized sector. This can probably be explained by the fact that during this period, despite weaker intervention by the central authorities, local authorities continued to exert pressure on enterprises to maintain a certain level of internal savings. Be that as it may, the experience of this laissez-faire period is too short to prove or disprove the validity of the Furubotn-Pejović prediction, and a full assessment of the theory on the basis of this experience is inconclusive.

Serious objections to the property right school of Furubotn-Pejović can also be made on theoretical and logical grounds. Branko Horvat rejects their explanation of the low propensity to save in the self-managed firm, finding it theoretically inconsistent and contradictory to Yugoslav reality. He questions the idea that in the Yugoslav firm the worker gets a profit on his collective saving only equal to the interest rate, while as a consumer, when he saves a part of his individual income, he gets interest without parting with his principal. What is overlooked, according to Horvat, is that the worker pays taxes on his income before depositing it in the bank, while the firm pays no taxes on the part of income which is saved. Another point stressed by Horvat is the behavioral inconsistency of the Furubotn-Pejović effect. To make their argument consistent, he points out, we would need to observe the following phenomena: (a) when the profit rate is not sufficiently high to cover the consumer interest rate and the loss of principal, calculated over the planning horizon, worker-managers stop saving collectively and distribute the entire income in wages; (b) on the other hand, when the situation is reversed, in particular when the consumer interest rate is negative, consumers stop depositing their money in banks and everything is saved collectively. But nothing of the sort has been observed. Consumers save even when the interest rate is negative; and even when it is highly positive, they still do not stop saving collectively. Horvat argues that the low propensity to save by the self-management firm has nothing to do with the Furubotn-Pejović property rights concept, but rather with misguided financial policies in Yugoslavia, which make the firm's behavior in saving relatively little very rational: "Why should they save more if they can finance the desired investment—very large by any standard, anyhow. Low saving can easily be explained by high inflation and negative interest rates."[29] Bank credit is a form of subsidy that substantially limits the risk involved in the investment process. Thus the enterprises can have their cake and eat it too. That is to say, they can use their net output for consumption, while borrowing money to finance investment under very favorable conditions and weak enforcement of loan repayment in case of financial difficulties.

In our view, however, the most fundamental shortcoming of the property rights school of Furubotn-Pejović lies not so much in logical inconsistencies or unrealistic assumptions, but rather in their rejection of the possibility that the indicated weaknesses in the property relations of self-management can be overcome within the framework of this system.[30] According to them, nothing short of private property of the means of production can remedy the major shortcomings of the Yugoslav economy. In our opinion this is debatable at the very least. Even if we assume, as the above-mentioned authors do, that the time horizon of workers in self-managed firms is short and the rate of return not high enough to compensate for the loss of principal, there are remedies short of granting the workers a transferable right of ownership in the net worth of the firm; for example, a sort of lump sum bonus, the size of which would be linked with length of service, to be paid upon retirement or when the worker leaves the enterprise.

Variations of this idea have been suggested by several other authors. For example, Šik proposed that all employees receive a certificate entitling them to participate in the profit of the enterprise, and to continue receiving dividends even after they retire.[31] The certificates would not be inheritable and would not circulate on the market. After the death of the owner the certificates return to the enterprise. In case of change of workplace, the employee is obligated to sell his certificates at official prices. At the new place of work he must start from the beginning to build up his or her ownership certificate assets. The weak side of this proposal is a lack of specification of how to assess the value of the certificates.

Addressing the same problem, economists in Yugoslavia like Madžar propose the creation of "a workers' fund." Employees of the self-managed firm would create a "workers' fund" out of their personal incomes. This fund would be set aside for accumulation and should constitute approximately 30% of the value of the firm's assets. Workers who leave the firm would be able to take their share of the funds with them. If the firm suffers a loss, the "workers' fund" would decline and the firm would cease to be self-managed until the "workers' fund" was built up again. In this way a sort of quasi-ownership in the assets of the firm would give the workers an interest in proper care of the capital stock.

Parenthetically, we consider it unfortunate that the radical reformers in Eastern Europe, and particularly in Hungary,[32] have rejected the Yugoslav experience of self-management as not very promising for creating a viable socialist economic system. Instead, they look for solutions in a full-fledged market economy (including a well-developed capital market) and in the pluralization of property forms (private, cooperative, municipal, etc.). The radical market reformers propose that large concerns should be denationalized and turned into joint stock companies. Under this specific property arrangement the stockholders would be enterprises and firms, banks, insurance companies, municipalities, universities, other associations, and even individuals. These stockholding institutions, and not the working collectives, would control the entrepreneurial functions. Self-management organizations, if created, would cooperate with management and share power in decision making in some areas of economic activity, along the lines practiced by some large West German firms.

In some respects the radical reformers' criticism of the existing Yugoslav self-management system is justified, especially when it comes to the failure of the system to internalize social property by the workers as their own. They are correct in pointing out that the Yugoslav self-management system has not produced a full-blooded owner of capital, but, instead, public property, which in Yugoslavia as in any other socialist country is nobody's property and gets treated accordingly. At the same time, however, the negative Yugoslav experience cannot be assumed to mean that a radical change in property relations is not possible under labor self-management conditions *per se*, or that workers are incapable of internalizing social property as their own and becoming interested in the net worth of the capital assets of their firm. Even a certain segment of the property rights school in the West will grant that the shortcomings of the property relations in the Yugoslav self-management system can be overcome without giving the workers full property rights over net worth.[33] This is why economists, both in the East and in the West, have proposed some changes in the Yugoslav property regime that would grant the workers limited property rights without abolishing self-management.

Finally, the property rights school, despite certain disputable aspects of its theory, especially in its extreme variant, has addressed a number of important problems regarding the role of property relations in the allocation of resources, the behavioral implications of incentives, the possibility of creating a capital market in socialism, and the exercise of control over the proper use of capital in enterprises.

It has also drawn attention to the workers' lack of interest in financing the growth of capital assets out of their income. A substantial number of Yugoslav economists and some state authorities support certain changes in property relations in light of certain weakness indicated by the property rights school.[34]

CHAPTER V

Conclusions:
Is Self-Management the Villain?

In this last chapter an attempt will be made to rethink and reconsider the main factors contributing to the apparent interbranch wage differentials in Yugoslavia, differentials which have been ably noted in the literature and especially by the advocates of the three schools presented in the previous chapter. We will then conclude with a summary of the main findings of this brief study.

The three schools reviewed in our work, although they take different approaches to the causes of interbranch differentials, have something in common: they link those differentials with the nature of the Yugoslav self-management system. They all argue, directly or indirectly, that the absence of both labor and capital markets is a *sine qua non* of the Yugoslav self-management system, and at the same limits the mobility of both factors of production. The use of neoclassical general equilibrium tools allows the adherents of the various schools to prove that under these circumstances interbranch and interfirm differentials are bound to be specific; that certain industries and firms will pay higher wages than others for the same occupation or job.

But the question to be raised here is this: Are these differentials specific to the Yugoslav type of self-management? We can convincingly argue that the phenomenon of substantial differences in wages for the same occupation, job, etc., is not specific to the Yugoslav self-management system, but rather to any market economy,[1] whether it is self-managed or not. What is more, in Yugoslavia certain non-systemic factors are also at work that contribute to the existence of such differences. Let us elaborate on these points.

In the neoclassical world, the argument goes, wages provide incentives for labor mobility. Shifts in product demand lead to transitory wage differentials, reflecting current differences in labor productivity. These differentials, however, are not destined to last for long. Wage equilibrium for the same job or occupation is bound to be reached. The "transitory" wage differentials initiate a flow of workers from low productivity/low wage sectors to high productivity/high wage sectors, a flow that will, in the long run, ensure the equalization of productivity and wages among branches and firms for the same job or occupation. In this "ideal" world, wage differentials associated with a specific industry are bound to disappear sooner or later, together with unemployment, precisely because wages adjust themselves until the demand for workers equals supply. This equalization brings, in effect, a clearing in the labor market. It is worth emphasizing here that in this line of reasoning unemployment is linked with wage dispersion; or, to put it in different terms, unemployment results when wages are above the marginal productivity of labor.

If there is a shortcoming with this line of reasoning, it is that the reality defies it. We know all too well that in reality interbranch differentials in the developed capitalist countries are anything but transitory. On the contrary, they have a tendency to persist for long periods of time.

A brief survey of the relevant literature testifies to the validity of this point. Kruger and Summers, Dickens and Katz, among others,[2] have accumulated impressive evidence showing that in the United States the impact of industry affiliation on wage differentials is not just significant but very large indeed. Available figures from 1984 indicate wide-ranging differentials from a high of 38% above the mean in the petroleum industry to a low of 37% below the mean in private household services. Sizable wage differentials for the same job were found in September 1985 in Cleveland,[3] where a key-entry operator's wages ranged from $160 to $480 per week.

The data also indicate a similarity in the wage structures of various developed capitalist countries and a remarkable stability of those structures over time. Moreover, the differences are not characteristic only of very specific jobs or occupations, but are evident in all jobs and professions. Certain industries pay higher wages not only to their highly skilled employees, but to clerks and unskilled workers as well, whereas others pay everybody low wages. As a result, in all industries the relative differences in wages for various skills and occupations or between men and women are more or less the same and show very little tendency to change over the long run.

Bringing together the findings from our statistical analysis of the wage structure in Yugoslavia (see chapter II) and findings on wage differences in capitalist countries, we can conclude that in both cases wages for the same job or occupation tend to differ a great deal by branch and enterprise. In other words, such wage differentials are as widespread a phenomenon in capitalist countries as they are in Yugoslavia. This would suggest that the competitive neoclassical approach cannot satisfactorily explain interbranch differentials either in Yugoslavia or in capitalist countries.

It seems to us that the neoclassical analysis overlooks the fact that any system in which remuneration is linked in one way or another with the actual economic results of the enterprise, measured by profitability or net output, or for that matter by any other economic indicator such as market share, is bound to create differences in wages for the same occupation in different branches and enterprises. The mere fact that labor productivity and market conditions are different for different branches and enterprises practically guarantees that wage differentials cannot be equalized as the neoclassical textbook analysis would have us believe.

Be that as it may, the fact that substantial differentials in pay for the same job or occupation persist in Yugoslavia and in many capitalist countries raises the question: What contributes to these differentials? Two theoretical approaches to this question demand our attention: the efficiency wage theory and the fair wage theory.

The premise of the efficiency wage concept is that labor exchange is open-ended. Particular work activities and work intensity are not specified in the labor contract. These aspects of labor activity are determined by the ability of the employer to exercise authority over the employees. In many cases, firms may deliberately set wages above the market clearing level in order to encourage greater work effort, and to reduce turnover which is disruptive to the operation of the firm. But these are not the only reasons for higher wages. They also attract superior applicants, allow the firm to retain the workers it has, and, most importantly, they provide the necessary incentive to workers in key positions to perform better. Overall, the efficiency wage theory holds that firms, in some respects, are not wage takers but wage makers, because wages are not something externally given to them, but rather are controlled by the firm as a determining factor contributing to higher productivity. We can deduce from this that the relationship between wages and productivity is a reciprocal one: high productivity determines high wages and high wages determine high productivity. This in turn implies that over some range, increases in wages may very well raise the profits of a firm, because it is reasonable to expect that in some firms[4] costs will increase less than the increase in productivity.[5]

The followers of the fair wage theory share some of the views expressed by the efficiency wage theory school, but raise objections to some other aspects of their theory. For instance, they share the view that high wages in some industries affect productivity positively without reducing profits. They also accept the argument that high wages paid to induce effort and discipline are usually above the clearing wage. On the other hand, fair wage theory advocates find that the efficiency wage theory does not explain the fact that all employees in the high wage industries are paid relatively higher wages, even in those jobs where efficiency wage elements are not important. While it may be understandable that a skilled machine operator receives a wage premium, it is not so clear why clerks and unskilled workers in the highly paid industries receive such premiums. The adherents of the fair wage concept[6] therefore propose an amendment to the efficiency wage concept, namely that all workers in certain industries are paid high wages because this is considered fair.

This last point brings into focus another important concern: Which firms and industries are able to pay relatively high wages and what are the factors determining an industry's ability to pay high wages? The predominant view shared by both schools mentioned above is that high wages are usually paid in industries that manifest the following characteristics: they have substantial market power; are made up of large firms with large establishments; have high union density; have high capital-labor ratios; and employ fewer women. At the other end of the pay spectrum, of course, are those industries with the opposite characteristics. It is striking that the characteristics of industries paying high and low wages (except for density of unionization) also apply to Yugoslav firms.

However, the mere fact that interbranch differentials for the same occupations do exist both in Yugoslavia and in the developed capitalist countries does not entirely invalidate the claim made by the previously reviewed schools, and the labor school in particular, that Yugoslavia is, after all, specific in this matter, as long as it can be proven that those differentials are visibly larger in Yugoslavia than in the developed capitalist countries. This is exactly what Estrin, one of the prominent representatives of the labor school, tried to prove, with little success. He used the coefficient of variation measure for international comparisons of interbranch differentials. This measure, however, is not without reproach, mainly because the size of this coefficient depends on the number of branches in the sample and the weight of different industrial branches, not to mention the exact definitions of branches. Needless to say, these factors differ significantly between Yugoslavia and the Western economies. But, even overlooking, for the sake of argument, the questionable usefulness of the coefficient of variation for international comparisons, available statistical data for the United States presented by Estrin himself do not indicate any substantial differences in interbranch differentials measured by this tool between that country and Yugoslavia. In fact Estrin's data indicate that the United States have a coefficient of variation at least as high as Yugoslavia's, if not higher.[7]

Reflecting on the issues and arguments raised in the previous pages, we can conclude that the self-management system in Yugoslavia is probably not the main cause of substantial interbranch differentials. Our analysis points to the fact that this phenomenon is rather linked with the Yugoslav decentralized coordinating mechanism—the market—as well as with other factors not linked, at least not directly, with the economic system itself.

More precisely, our analysis suggests that in Yugoslavia, more than in many other countries, some distributional phenomena are not entirely systemically determined. We can point out at once a few aspects of the distributional pattern that cannot be linked with systemic characteristics. For example, state economic policies in the field of distribution, which are not in conformity with the requirement or logic of the system, cannot be attributed to systemic inadequacies alone. It is practically impossible for anyone to determine unambiguously which elements of state policy can be attributed to the logic of the system and which are alien to it. The arbitrariness in this matter is very evident when the state decides to redistribute income, as is the case in Yugoslavia. The self-management reward system, in an environment of imperfect competition, sometimes allows gains in net personal incomes which are unrelated to the overall effort and performance of a particular enterprise. There is then an ideological and practical effort by the state to skim the unjustified incomes via taxes and other monetary and fiscal tools.[8] But, given the very nature of the system, no objective criteria can be worked out to separate justified from unjustified income without undermining the self-management market system itself. Thus, in practice, exhortations that enterprises should be rewarded according to their contributions in terms of labor can mean only an arbitrary use of the tax system. The state authorities are the final judge in deciding which incomes are earned and which are not.

The specific and important role of the state in this matter must, however, be seen in conjunction with a multitude of sociopolitical factors, many of which are not quantifiable, which have played some role in determining the dispersion of wages. It must be emphasized here that the economic and social policies of the Yugoslav state are strongly shaped by regional diversity, underdevelopment, and the need to protect the communist party's monopoly on power. In addition, ideology and certain strong biases held by the communist regime have strongly influenced economic policies. As is the case in other East European socialist countries, the elite in power has a strong mistrust and fear of uncontrolled market forces; a fascination with bigness; a bias in favor of material production; and a fear that if nonlabor income is allowed it will lead to capitalism.

The reluctance of the state to modify the property relations even slightly is another example of deep-rooted ideological concerns and fears. The major fear of the authorities is that incomes from property will create a class of rentiers and increase the stratification of society. The experience of the capitalist world, from its very early stages, justifies this fear. Income from property is more unequally distributed and tends to be more concentrated in comparison with income from employment, and thus adds a new dimension to social stratification. Furthermore, the implementation of property rights requires, in one form or another, the creation of a genuine capital market in which firms can participate directly. There is, however, no historical experience of the creation of an institutionalized genuine market within the framework of public ownership. The most relevant case at hand is the Yugoslav experience after 1965, when investment allocation was decentralized and enterprises were encouraged to use banks—

which were supposedly independent of the state—as a sort of capital market. As we have already shown, the results were disappointing.

A further expression of ideology and strong bias against the market is the state's far-reaching intervention in product markets. In Yugoslavia, product markets and specialty markets of factors of production are seriously limited by state intervention. These barriers and limits are much more extensive than in the most developed capitalist countries with the highest levels of state intervention. Even in the 1965-72 period, the heyday of liberalism, when the scope of market forces was substantially broader and before the so-called social agreements were introduced, approximately 50% to 60% of all prices in industry were directly or indirectly controlled by the federal, republican, or local authorities.[9]

As far as income distribution is concerned, the state has always had some control over the wage differentials. Formally, in accordance with the theoretical construct of a market self-managed economy, the state plays no role in establishing either interskill or interbranch differentials. The only parameter of distribution is the federal minimum wage; the rest is left to the discretion of the enterprises on a micro level and to the market on a macro level. But in reality this is far from the truth. The state has intervened both directly and indirectly in the distributional pattern. With the exception of the laissez-faire period between 1965 and 1970, when most restrictions on income distribution were abolished, the state, indirectly through its price policies, has affected (not always by design) the interbranch and interfirm differentials by granting certain industries privileges in the form of subsidies, credit, and tax exemptions. A good case in point is the direct intervention by the state in 1972 in both interskill and interbranch differentials in order to curb dispersion of wages. The right of the enterprises to distribute income was substantially reduced. Although some of the restrictions, especially on skill differentials, were abolished after 1975, social contracts on prices, income distribution, and other economic parameters have influenced the interbranch and interfirm differentials ever since. Although a lack of real coordination of the enormous number of social contracts made it impossible to implement any desired objectives on a national scale as far as interbranch differentials are concerned (even if such an objective could be formulated clearly, which is not always the case), state intervention in this field is not neutral. By granting certain branches and enterprises special treatment for whatever reason, the state *nolens volens* affects the wage differentials of those entities.

Not without importance in this matter is the lobbying power of particular branches and firms to achieve concessions from the state in the form of subsidies, tax exemptions, favorable credit conditions, etc. Those concessions are very often more important for the economic performance of the enterprise than its own "internal" effort.

Regional diversity has also played some role in shaping the overall interbranch differentials. As our statistical analysis indicates, interbranch differentials are larger in underdeveloped regions than in the more developed ones. This phenomenon can probably be explained by the logic of underdevelopment; a greater scarcity of skilled manpower and a greater abundance of unskilled workers will *ceteris paribus* produce larger pay differentials in preferential branches and firms than will be the case in the more developed regions. In any case, the regional element adds some new dimension to the inequality of pay.

Whatever the reasons for large interbranch and interfirm differentials, they have serious negative consequences, because they lead to a situation in which what you do is not as important as where you do it. The level of wages for a particular job depends more on what region, branch, or firm you work in than on your qualifications, skills, and responsibilities. There can be no doubt that this does not accord with the sacred principle of distribution according to work.

* * *

Reflecting on the information, data, and analysis presented thus far, we can draw the following conclusions. First, changes in the principles of income distribution, as well as changes in the self-management system, have evolved gradually as part of the historical process. It is equally true and noteworthy that enterprises gradually gained control, at least formally, over income distribution and income differentials, particularly after the 1961 and 1965 reforms. But these "rights" did not last very long and were withdrawn to some extent during the postreform period of the 1970s.

Second, our statistical analysis has shown that the Yugoslav system, in spite of marketization, has not increased social stratification. To the contrary, as in many other socialist countries, occupational differentials have actually declined during the last twenty years. According to all our statistical indicators, the overall level of inequality in Yugoslavia is low by Western standards and lower than in many Comecon countries (the USSR, Poland, and others). The increase in inequality of pay, both between skills and between branches, after the introduction of the market-oriented economic reform of 1965 does not provide decisive evidence that this increase was a result of market forces, because the increase in dispersion of personal income was very short-lived (only three to four years) and was not very dramatic; in some republics there was no increase at all.

Third, the Yugoslav distributional pattern, as can be seen from our statistical analysis, is characterized by very low skill differentials on the one hand, and high levels of interbranch and interfirm differentials on the other. From an incentive point of view, this distributional pattern is very inefficient. Very often a worker's earnings do not depend on what he does but where he does it. Payment for the same jobs, skills, and occupations can differ substantially in different branches and enterprises.

Fourth, the neoclassical static equilibrium models used by different schools do not adequately explain the relatively large interbranch differentials in Yugoslavia. All the schools linked the relatively high interbranch differentials with the nature of the Yugoslav type of self-management, with the particular property regime. We do not deny that certain specific features of Yugoslav self-management, like low mobility of capital and labor, have some influence on income distribution, but in our opinion it is not specific to self-management of the Yugoslav type or to any self-management system. We observe this phenomenon to a significant degree in all Western-oriented market economies. We are, therefore, inclined to link the large interbranch differentials in Yugoslavia with the decentralized market mechanism, to the extent that such mechanism is operative, and to nonsystemic factors, especially state intervention.

Finally, let us consider the reasons for the overall egalitarian trend in income distribution and its particular distributional pattern, and whether or not this can be explained by the economic system *per se* or by its self-management character. Our study has gone a long way toward indicating which systemic and nonsystemic factors can possibly explain income distribution phenomena in Yugoslavia. We have done this always keeping in mind the inherent difficulty in distinguishing which elements of the economic system (for example the market *per se* or its specific self-managed form) can be linked to certain phenomena of income distribution, as well as the difficulty in distinguishing between the influence of the economic system and the economic policy of the state on income distribution, and even more, which elements of state policy are deliberate and which are unexpected or undesired results. As far as skill differentials are concerned, their low level and tendency to decline in the long run cannot be explained in terms of the Yugoslav self-management system.

This egalitarian tendency is, in our opinion, not specific to self-management in general, or to the Yugoslav variety in general. Even if we assume that self-managed enterprises may not require such high differentials to motivate employees to good work as enterprises without industrial participatory democracy, because other more noble compensating incentives can be used, this by itself does not mean that the Yugoslav self-managed system has produced such compensating incentives. Indeed, sociological surveys indicate that this is not the case. Genuine self-management in Yugoslavia is still just a desideratum, very far from reality.

We are inclined to argue that low skill differentials in Yugoslavia are linked with the egalitarian ethos that has taken root in that country. This part of the socialist ideology, unlike others (e.g., internalization of social property as one's own, individual work as work for the community, etc.), has succeeded, and is considered as one of the indispensable features of socialism. The workers in the enterprise, together with the party elite, are the guardians of egalitarian skill differentials. But this egalitarian trend has its negative consequences for the possibilities of systemic changes in Yugoslavia. A point can be made here that the failure of the reforms to increase inequalities substantially signifies a failure of the reforms in general. Although the failure of the Yugoslav experiment may have multiple causes, it is our opinion that one of them is the failure to motivate workers, through a more differentiated pay system, to work more efficiently. Some could argue, and rightly so, that factors other than equality are important causes of the systemic failures. Among these are the inability of the system to harden the budget constraints; to change property relations; to prevent preferential treatment of some branches by political authorities; and to democratize political life. It is hardly necessary to say that these factors are of paramount importance for the failure of the reforms. However, it is doubtful that the degree of inequality of pay can be treated entirely as an independent variable vis-à-vis some of these other factors. The degree of inequality influences, for example, the degree of softness of the budget constraints. Hardening of the budget constraints would require some unemployment, resulting in a relative decline of pay for the less skilled employees, and would also require the dismissal of the less skilled and the low achievers from the enterprises. After all, what is the concept of hard budget constraints but a requirement to save on inputs in general and on the labor input in particular, in order to increase profitability? For this objective to be achieved, however, pay must be differentiated to a greater degree than it is now, in order to motivate better work.

Appendix

Table A

Distribution of Net Personal Income in the Socialized Sector in Republics and Provinces, 1964–1976 (measures of dispersion)

In the republics and autonomous provinces

	In all Yugoslavia						Bosnia-Herzegovina						Montenegro					
	$\frac{P_{99}}{P_1}$	$\frac{P_{98}}{P_2}$	$\frac{P_{95}}{P_5}$	$\frac{P_{90}}{P_{10}}$	V	Gini	$\frac{P_{99}}{P_1}$	$\frac{P_{98}}{P_2}$	$\frac{P_{95}}{P_5}$	$\frac{P_{90}}{P_{10}}$	V	Gini	$\frac{P_{99}}{P_1}$	$\frac{P_{98}}{P_2}$	$\frac{P_{95}}{P_5}$	$\frac{P_{90}}{P_{10}}$	V	Gini
1964	7.1	5.4	3.8	2.8	46.0	0.23	5.8	4.7	3.5	2.7	44.3	0.22	8.5	6.0	4.1	3.0	49.2	0.25
1966	8.1	5.7	3.9	2.8	45.6	0.23	7.3	5.2	3.6	2.7	44.0	0.22	10.0	6.5	4.0	2.9	46.9	0.24
1967	8.7	6.2	4.1	2.9	46.8	0.24	8.4	5.9	3.9	2.9	46.4	0.23	10.9	7.1	4.2	3.0	48.2	0.24
1969	8.3	5.9	4.0	2.9	47.7	0.24	7.2	5.2	3.7	2.8	45.4	0.23	8.9	5.9	3.9	2.8	45.4	0.23
1971	7.0	5.5	3.9	2.8	47.0	0.23	6.3	5.1	3.7	2.7	45.4	0.23	6.1	5.1	3.7	2.7	44.2	0.22
1972	7.0	5.1	3.7	2.7	45.4	0.23	5.8	4.8	3.5	2.7	44.2	0.22	5.9	4.8	3.5	2.6	42.2	0.21
1973	6.2	5.0	3.6	2.7	44.3	0.22	5.8	4.8	3.5	2.6	43.3	0.22	5.4	4.5	3.5	2.6	41.5	0.21
1974	6.1	4.8	3.4	2.6	43.0	0.21	5.7	4.6	3.4	2.6	42.8	0.21	5.4	4.4	3.3	2.6	41.3	0.21
1975	6.2	4.8	3.4	2.6	42.9	0.21	5.9	4.7	3.4	2.6	42.5	0.21	5.6	4.3	3.3	2.6	41.6	0.21
1976	6.1	4.9	3.5	2.6	42.7	0.21	5.8	4.7	3.4	2.6	42.5	0.21	6.0	4.7	3.5	2.6	42.8	0.22

	Serbia Proper*						Vojvodina						Kosovo					
	$\frac{P_{99}}{P_1}$	$\frac{P_{98}}{P_2}$	$\frac{P_{95}}{P_5}$	$\frac{P_{90}}{P_{10}}$	V	Gini	$\frac{P_{99}}{P_1}$	$\frac{P_{98}}{P_2}$	$\frac{P_{95}}{P_5}$	$\frac{P_{90}}{P_{10}}$	V	Gini	$\frac{P_{99}}{P_1}$	$\frac{P_{98}}{P_2}$	$\frac{P_{95}}{P_5}$	$\frac{P_{90}}{P_{10}}$	V	Gini
1964	7.3	5.3	3.7	2.7	45.2	0.22	6.3	4.8	3.4	2.5	44.0	0.21	14.9	8.8	4.8	3.2	56.1	0.27
1966	8.6	5.9	3.9	2.8	46.3	0.23	8.0	5.6	3.7	2.7	43.8	0.22	10.7	6.8	4.1	3.0	49.7	0.25
1967	9.7	6.4	4.1	2.9	47.0	0.24	10.8	6.9	4.1	2.8	46.4	0.23	9.1	6.1	3.9	2.8	46.8	0.24
1969	9.1	6.1	4.0	2.8	47.9	0.24	8.0	5.5	3.8	2.7	46.0	0.23	9.7	6.2	3.9	2.8	46.9	0.23
1971	6.8	5.5	3.9	2.8	47.6	0.24	6.7	5.2	3.7	2.7	46.0	0.23	6.1	5.1	3.6	2.7	45.8	0.22
1972	6.6	5.2	3.7	2.7	45.9	0.23	6.1	4.8	3.5	2.6	43.4	0.21	6.0	4.8	3.4	2.5	43.1	0.21
1973	6.4	5.0	3.7	2.7	45.5	0.23	6.0	4.8	3.5	2.6	44.0	0.22	6.5	4.8	3.4	2.5	44.1	0.21
1974	6.2	4.8	3.5	2.6	43.4	0.22	6.1	4.8	3.4	2.6	42.9	0.21	5.8	4.6	3.4	2.5	42.8	0.21
1975	6.3	4.9	3.5	2.6	43.5	0.22	6.3	4.9	3.4	2.6	42.5	0.21	5.6	4.4	3.3	2.5	42.7	0.21
1976	6.2	5.0	3.6	2.7	44.0	0.22	6.0	4.8	3.5	2.6	42.3	0.21	6.2	4.8	3.5	2.6	43.9	0.22

Source: Statistical Yearbook of Yugoslavia (SGJ).

See notes to Table 1.

*Considering that Serbia consists of Serbia proper and 2 autonomous provinces—Vojvodina and Kosovo—which are independent administrative units not very different in their prerogatives from republics, we treat them as separate units of analyses like all other republics. Besides, including Kosovo as a separate unit is also useful, due to the fact that it is the most backward region of Yugoslavia, and thus allows a comparison of the extreme differences in pay (for example, Slovenia with Kosovo).

Table B

Dispersion of Skill Differentials in Republics and Provinces Measured by the Coefficient of Variation (V)

	All Yugoslavia	Republics and autonomous provinces							
		Bosnia-Herzegovina	Montenegro	Croatia	Macedonia	Slovenia	Serbia Proper	Vojvodina	Kosovo
Socialized Economy									
1966	32.4	33.4	33.9	32.2	33.8	33.3	32.2	30.7	35.1
1967	34.3	34.3	33.6	34.3	36.6	36.0	34.4	34.0	37.1
1968	33.4	35.4	33.5	33.3	33.1	34.8	33.3	32.4	38.2
1969	33.9	36.4	32.0	32.9	35.6	34.5	34.1	33.3	37.0
1970	35.0	36.8	35.7	35.1	34.7	36.1	35.1	33.9	37.9
1971	34.4	36.6	35.5	33.8	34.4	34.6	33.3	31.8	33.4
1972	33.5	36.4	33.0	32.6	32.3	34.0	33.1	31.6	33.8
1973	32.0	35.0	32.1	30.9	30.1	31.6	31.3	30.0	34.2
1974	31.5	35.1	32.7	29.7	30.8	32.4	31.5	30.1	34.9
1976	30.9	33.9	32.8	29.9	30.2	30.7	31.5	30.3	33.4
Industry									
1966	34.0	34.9	36.6	33.6	35.5	34.8	34.6	33.6	40.1
1967	33.0	34.9	35.0	36.3	35.7	34.0	32.7	35.8	41.2
1968	32.3	35.3	33.8	33.1	31.5	37.0	31.5	33.5	46.3
1969	33.8	36.3	33.8	35.9	33.7	36.8	32.8	34.6	41.9
1970	37.0	38.5	37.9	35.8	35.0	38.3	37.8	34.3	43.4
1971	36.1	36.6	37.6	34.9	35.1	38.2	36.0	33.8	39.8
1972	34.8	36.6	34.2	33.3	33.3	37.5	34.7	35.5	38.5
1973	32.2	33.3	32.6	31.1	30.6	32.7	33.3	34.1	39.5
1974	32.1	34.9	32.4	31.1	30.0	32.7	32.4	33.8	41.2

Source: Statistical Yearbook of Yugoslavia (SGJ).

Notes

I. A Survey of Systemic Changes

1. For more details see E. Berković, "Differentiation of Personal Income," *Yugoslavia Survey*, 1971.

2. Data comparing immediate postwar differentials with the prewar old regime are scanty. Calculations done by T. Mulina and K. Mihailović in *Pitanje plata u FNRJ* [Wages in Yugoslavia] (Institute of Economics, Belgrade, Serbia) indicate much bigger differences in earnings between manual and nonmanual employees before than after the war. The figures are as follows:

	Manual workers = 100		Office employees in industry = 100	
Years	Office employees in industry	Civil servants	Manual workers	Civil servants
1939	175	193	57	111
1953	122	104	82	85

3. Under this system and during the first year, some enterprises ascribed fictitious rates to different skills in order to increase the "accountable wages." In 1955 all enterprises were obliged to discuss their wage scale schedules with trade unions and local governments; this was a sort of collective agreement.

4. Although wages out of profit vary, they have always been a rather small fraction of the combined total wage. According to H. M. Wachtel's calculations, the ratio of variable to fixed wages in industry has fluctuated between 8% and 15% for all employees. Even for the highest white-collar employees, for whom the ratio is substantially higher than the average, it has never exceeded 21% (for the years 1956, 1959, and 1961). See H. M. Wachtel, *Management and Workers' Wages in Yugoslavia: The Theory and Practice of Participatory Socialism* (Ithaca and London: Cornell University Press, 1975), p. 108, Table 5.1.

The ratio of variable wages to fixed wages in Yugoslavia does not differ very much from what is typical in other socialist countries, where premiums and bonuses likewise represent a rather small fraction of total earnings (and hence are not adequate stimuli for better work and innovations). See J. Adam, ed., *Employment Policies in the Soviet Union and Eastern Europe* (London: Macmillan, and New York: St. Martin's, 1982).

5. In 1952 the commune was established as the primary political unit. The 1953 Constitution gave communes the power to legislate in all matters except where the federation or the republics had exclusive authority. They have wide discretion to levy local taxes on enterprises, and often they tax efficient enterprises heavily, in order to finance the inefficient ones. The commune has substantial influence over the distribution of retained earnings. Enterprises are obliged to present their annual

plans to the commune for approval and policy recommendations, and seldom are those recommendations not accepted. In the case of investment projects financed with borrowed money, the commune has a substantial say because it acts as a guarantor to the bank. As far as the everyday activities of the enterprise are concerned, the communes exert influence through their power to hire and fire enterprise directors, which obviously motivates a director to be sensitive to the wishes of the commune.

The economic chambers established in 1954 are another, though less powerful, source of influence over the enterprises. Each economic sector is represented by a chamber, in which membership was made compulsory after 1958. The chamber's influence is similar to that of the commune, but is functional rather than territorial. Enterprises submit their production and investment plans to their chamber for scrutiny and recommendations, in order to avoid over- or underproduction or multiplication of capacities. But, as in the case of the commune, the recommendations of the chamber are not legally binding.

6. Although in many instances quite a few criteria were used to classify employees into different skill groups, in the centralism period the level of skill and work experience were most often the only criteria used for manual workers, whereas for nonmanual workers the level of education and work experience were used as criteria by most enterprises. The function of planning the enterprise's skill differentials for the next year was entrusted to the workers' council, whose proposals were then discussed and adopted by a general meeting of all the employees of the enterprise. Until 1961 the enterprise rules for wage distribution required the approval of the commune to become binding. Toward the end of the 1950s a more sophisticated job rating system was introduced. Each job was evaluated in terms of required skill, experience, and education, responsibility, physical effort, mental effort, working conditions, etc. For each of these criteria, points are awarded. However, as Wachtel reports from interviews with enterprise officials (see *Management and Workers' Wages in Yugoslavia*), the most important criteria in the assessment of points are the more measurable objective criteria of experience, skill, and education required. The preliminary structure based on this job evaluation may be adjusted to labor market conditions, for example by comparing it with the wage structures in other enterprises in the industry or in other enterprises in the same location.

7. The standard or calculated wage fund represents the wage fund that is based on wage rates for different skills set by the federal government. If the actual full wage fund of the enterprise exceeded the standard wage fund by more than 20%, a steep tax was levied on the wage fund. This progressive tax could be as high as 70% of the nonpermitted excess wage fund.

8. A tax on capital stock was first introduced in 1953. The tax rates were highly differentiated (between 0 and 6%) from industry to industry. The purpose of this instrument was to force enterprises to use capital prudently and at the same time to be a source for financing investment by the state. It should be stressed here that in the early 1950s enterprises were allowed to keep only a small percent of their accumulation fund, and even amortization funds were concentrated in the hands of the Federal Investment Fund (FIF). But gradually enterprise investment financed from the enterprises' own resources increased; by the end of the 1950s nearly 30% of all such investment was financed by the enterprises' own resources. In 1963 the Federal Investment Fund was abolished, its funds turned over to various banks (the only investment fund left to the federation was the fund for accelerated development

of the underdeveloped regions). Thereafter, the old investment regime changed considerably. Enterprises invested from their own resources and from bank loans based on commercial principles. Their fiscal obligations were substantially reduced, to facilitate accumulation. The capital tax was gradually reduced and then abolished altogether in the early 1970s, as were progressive and proportional taxes on enterprise net income. For more details see Ante Čičin-Šain and Neven Mates, ''The Development and Role of the Major Economic Policy Instruments in Yugoslavia 1952-1972,'' in *Socialism and Industrialization: A Comparison of Economic Systems in Poland, Yugoslavia, China and Cuba* (Frankfurt and New York: Campus Verlag, 1985).

9. Branko Horvat, *The Yugoslav Economic System* (White Plains: IASP [M. E. Sharpe], 1976), p. 164.

10. Before the 1965 reform, the federal government was responsible for financing not only many capital-intensive infrastructure projects, but also projects in the manufacturing and other productive sectors. The major fund to finance investment by the federation was the Federal Investment Fund. After 1964 the role of the federation in investment allocation was limited to the fund for the underdeveloped regions. The federal government would annually distribute funds amounting to nearly 2% of the national output of the developed regions to the underdeveloped regions for investment purposes. The main source of financing this fund was a tax on fixed assets (a 5% capital charge) and contributions from the more developed regions. There was a dramatic change in financing investment in fixed capital after 1964. Whereas in 1962 the federal state's contribution to the overall investment funds was nearly 60% and the rest was done by the enterprise's own funds (38%) and banks (3%), in 1966 the central government's share was only 16%, the internal funds of enterprises covered 46%, and banks' funds accounted for 39%. Thus the banks replaced the federal government as a serious source of accumulation. In the late 1960s and early 1970s they further increased their share, at the expense of self-financed enterprise accumulation. During this period over half of all investment in fixed capital was financed by the banks. See Horvat, *The Yugoslav Economic System*, p. 222, Table 28.

11. Of course, we should caution readers that formal control over income distribution by the enterprise is not the same as real control. In a Communist one-party system, the state has many instruments to control how income will be allocated, abrogating to some degree the formal prerogatives granted by the same state to the enterprises. Although after the reforms of 1965, state intervention in distribution matters was substantially reduced, it has never ceased entirely in any period in socialist Yugoslavia.

12. For more details regarding the reforms of 1965 see R. Bićanić, *Economic Policy in Socialist Yugoslavia* (Cambridge: Cambridge University Press, 1973).

13. In 1957 Bićanić characterized the new Yugoslav system, its aims and means, and its differences from the Soviet-type economy in the following ways:

(a) social ownership of the means of production as opposed to state ownership;

(b) decentralized social planning as opposed to central planning;

(c) reliance on the market mechanism as a basic mechanism of allocation of goods and services, as opposed to administrative allocation (markets for capital and labor were not envisaged);

(d) increased use of financial instruments;

(e) free distribution of available income by workers' councils in contradistinction to administrative fixed wages;

(f) decentralized and functional budgeting at all administrative levels, as opposed to an all-embracing state budget;

(g) restoration of consumer sovereignty;

(h) acceptance of private farming and freely organized cooperatives, and a rejection of compulsory collectivization.

See R. Bićanić, "Economic Growth under Centralized and Decentralized Planning: Yugoslavia, A Case Study," in *Economic Development and Cultural Change*, vol. 5, 1957, pp. 63-74.

14. Jose Mencinger, "The Yugoslav Economic System and Performance of the Economy in the Seventies and Early Eighties," in *Socialism and Industrialization* (Frankfurt/New York: Campus Verlag, 1985), p. 198.

15. Ibid.

16. For example, in Belgrade the average income per worker and personal income per worker were established on an *ex post* basis. The average statistical figures for the previous year were used and a certain calculated rate of growth was added on the basis of predictions. Slovenia was the only republic where this average was established *ex ante*.

17. For more details see S. Babić, "The Problem of Choosing Indicators of Efficiency in the Yugoslav Economic System 1976-1980," *Economic Analysis and Workers' Management*, vol. 16, 1982, pp. 347-68. Econometric calculations for 1980 made by Babić indicate that the correlation of personal incomes in different republics is very weak, the parameter (R) ranging from 0.31 to 0.40 for 1980.

18. In Yugoslavia taxes are levied on gross personal income, but not as an aggregate percentage of gross personal income. Every item to be financed (such as education, health, sports, etc.) is covered by a separate tax as a percentage of gross personal income. For example, out of a total tax rate of 30%, 10% is to finance health, 10% education, etc.

19. The more prosperous republics usually oppose any federal interference in their economic affairs as incompatible with the democratic principle of decentralization, but in their own backyards they do not practice what they preach.

20. The Constitution of 1974 distinguishes two types of agreements: (a) self-management agreements made between buyers and sellers; and (b) social compact agreements, which are those in which some level of government is a participant. For example, the distribution of income is regulated by agreements between local or republican authorities, trade unions, chambers of commerce, etc.

21. For more details see Mencinger, "The Yugoslav Economic System and Performance of the Economy in the Seventies and Early Eighties."

22. See C. H. Prout, *Market Socialism in Yugoslavia* (Oxford: Oxford University Press, 1985).

23. Some economists claim that the Constitution of 1974 is the main cause of all Yugoslavia's ills. The constitution strengthened the autonomy of the republics and provinces, while at the same time it weakened the federal government and destroyed the unity of the Yugoslav market. This point of view is strongly expressed by Zagreb University professor Jovan Mirić in "The System and the Crisis," *Borba* (Belgrade), 12-25 October, 1984. The essays published by Mirić have stirred a lively controversy between the centralizers, strongly supported by the Serbian establishment, and opponents of centralization, mainly represented by Slovenian and Croatian officials and economists. However, in spite of all the criticism, to date no one in the

establishment, not even the most federally minded, has yet asked formally for the abolition of the 1974 Constitution, although of late there are more and more voices, especially in Serbia, openly calling for a new constitution.

24. As a result of the broad objectives of the "Long-Term Program of Economic Stabilization," several practical measures were proposed in 1984 and 1985. Some of the most important ones are the following:

(a) More severe administrative sanctions (in the form of limits on personal incomes) are to be imposed against enterprises with losses.

(b) A price freeze established in 1980 was abolished in 1984, and the market principles of price formation were to be enhanced. Price controls are supposed to be limited only to telephone and other communication rates, to railroad transport rates, energy prices, etc.

(c) Interest rates for credit are supposed to be higher than the inflation rate.

(d) In the summer of 1985 the Associated Labor Act of 1976 was seriously modified. Certain prerogatives of the "basic organization of associated labor" (a subfirm unit within the framework of the larger firm) were reduced. These measures aim to avoid fragmentation of the firms' economic activities and to improve the planning process of coordination both within the firm and at higher levels of economic activity. However, stiff opposition to the implementation of these measures has forced the authorities to postpone some of them several times or to mitigate them substantially.

II. Statistical Analysis

1. The existing official statistical materials in Yugoslavia allow us to compute a variety of inequality measures. In most cases, statistical data about personal incomes in branches and sectors, occupations and skills, are published in a systematic way. The category of wages has been replaced by the category of personal income in the official Yugoslav statistics. The gross income or total revenue of the firm, minus material cost, including amortization and legal and contractual obligations, is the net output (or income) of the firm, which in turn is divided into personal income and internal funds. Personal income, after deduction of income taxes and social security funds, is the sum paid out to the workers. Personal income as used in Yugoslav statistics is net of taxes and social security funds.

2. We do not analyze the years prior to 1964 because in the official statistical data the nomenclature, the number of branches in industry, and the classification of skill differentials are not the same as in the years after 1964.

3. For example, in 1967 employees of the Chamber of Commerce on the average received nearly 40% and banking employees 23% more personal income than employees in the nonmaterial sector in total (according to data from SGJ 1968).

4. See Henryk Flakierski, *Economic Reform and Income Distribution: A Case Study of Hungary and Poland* (Armonk: M. E. Sharpe, 1986), Tables 1 and 6; and for the Soviet Union, Jan Adam, ed., *Employment Policies in the Soviet Union and Eastern Europe* (London: Macmillan, and New York: St. Martin's, 1982).

In the Soviet Union distributional frequencies are still a strictly guarded secret. Only from time to time is a social economist permitted to reveal the "secret" and publish the decile ratios for some years in the form of a ready statement, without giving the frequency distributions from which they were computed. According to

N. E. Rabkina and N. M. Rimashevskaia ("Raspredelitel'nye otnosheniia i sotsial'noe razvitie" [Distributional Relations and Social Development], in *EKO* [Novosibirsk], 1978, no. 5, p. 20) and E. Fedorovskaia and E. Alexandrova (in "Mekhanizm formirovaniia i vozvysheniia potrebnostei" [The Mechanism of Forming and Increasing Needs], in *Voprosy ekonomiki*, 1984, no. 1, pp. 15-25), the decile ratios in the socialized sector were as follows: 1964—3.69; 1966—3.26; 1968—2.83; 1972—3.10; 1976—3.35; 1981—3.00. Comparing these figures with the figures in our Table 1 (see the ratio P_{90}/P_{10} in Table 1), we find that for all years the decile ratios in the USSR are higher than those in Yugoslavia.

The decile ratio is the ratio of the highest earnings in the bottom 90% of earnings to the highest earnings in the bottom 10% of earnings. The decile ratio can also be expressed as the ratio of the highest earnings in the ninth decile group to the highest earnings in the first decile group. In short, it is the ratio of the ninth to the first decile (D_9/D_1).

5. Sources: V. Pilić, *Karakteristike i problemi ženske radne snage u Jugoslaviji* [The Characteristics and Problems of the Female Labor Force in Yugoslavia] (Belgrade: Institut za ekonomska istraživanja [Institute of Economic Research], 1969), p. 89, and *Statistički bilten 788* (Belgrade: Savezni Zavod za Statistiku [Central Statistical Office], 1973).

6. For more details see Tea Petrin and Jane Humpries, "Women in the Self-Managed Economy of Yugoslavia," *Economic Analysis and Workers' Management*, vol. 14, no. 1 (1980), pp. 69-91.

7. Source: *Popis prebivalstva in stanovanj u letu 1971* [Census on the Structure of Employment Positions in 1971] (Belgrade: Savezni Zavod za Statistiku [Central Statistical Office], 1974).

8. See L. E. Kunelskii, *Zarobotnaia plata i stimulirovaniia truda* [Wages and Work Incentives] (Moscow, 1981).

9. See E. Berković in *Ekonomska politika*, no. 1709 (1984), p. 26.

10. The interbranch coefficient of variation (%) in Poland's industries are as follows: 1960—14.7%; 1970—15.2%; 1975—13.7%; 1979—12.0%; 1980—12.5% (see P. Dominiak, "Miedzydziatowe rozpietośći plać [Interbranch Pay Differentials], in *Życie gospodarcze*, no. 50 (December 11, 1983). International comparisons of interbranch differentials measured by the coefficient of variation are not without reproach since the size of the coefficient depends on the number of industries in the sample, the exact definitions of branches, etc. This qualification is, however, much more valid for comparisons of Western countries than for East European ones, because the classification of different branches of industry is very similar in Yugoslavia and the other East European countries.

11. For more details see S. Estrin, *Self-Management: Economic Theory and Yugoslav Practice* (Cambridge: Cambridge University Press, 1983), chapters 5 and 6 and Appendix B, Tables B5 and B6.

12. Ibid., chapter 5.

13. M. Popović and B. Sefer, "Analiza ličnih dohodaka po zanimanjimi u Beogradskoj privredi" [Analysis of Personal Incomes According to Occupation in the Belgrade Economy] in *Lični Dohoci* [Personal Income] (Belgrade: Saveza Sindicata Jugoslavije [The Center of Trade Unions of Yugoslavia], 1986), p. 21.

14. Estrin (in *Self-Management*, pp. 142-47) has approximated interfirm differentials within branches (in his usage—sectors) on the basis of pay of firms grouped according to size (in terms of net product, size of capital assets, and labor employed).

His findings for six years corroborate the existence of very large interfirm differentials in all industries. In 1966 only 4% of all firms had a difference in pay of less than 150%; two-thirds of all firms showed a difference in excess of 200%. A sizable minority had a difference in excess of 300% for four out of six years. In some single years the extreme was as high as 1500%.

15. According to our calculations the relative dispersion of pay for the fifteen Soviet republics (measured by the coefficient of variation and the ratio of extremes) is as follows, calculated on the basis of *Narodnoe khoziaistvo SSSR za 60 let* [The National Economy of the USSR for 60 Years], Moscow, 1977):

	1965	1970	1975
Coefficient of variation (%)	6.6	7.8	9.6
Ratio of the highest to the lowest paid republic	127	132	139

Source: Calculated on the basis of *Narodnoe khoziaistvo SSSR za 60 let* [The National Economy of the USSR for a period of 60 years] Moscow 1977.

16. The differences between personal incomes in the socialized and in the private agricultural sectors have a regional dimension. While specific geographical conditions have a very strong influence on success in agricultural production, those conditions do not coincide with the administrative regional divisions of republics and autonomous provinces. Hence, the relative ranking of republics and provinces in terms of average personal income in the socialized sector will be different from the relative ranking of administrative units according to their personal income in the private agricultural sector.

17. See E. Primorac, *Systemic and Policy Changes in Yugoslavia and Their Effect on Employment, 1953-1983* (paper delivered in Guelph at a conference sponsored by the Ontario Learned Societies, 1984).

18. B. Vuscović, ''Social Inequality in Yugoslavia,'' *New Left Review*, no. 95, pp. 26-45.

III. Skill Differentials and Self-Management

1. The claim regarding the abolishment of wage labor and the labor market in Yugoslavia after the introduction of a full-fledged self-management system is more a theoretical desideratum than a reflection of contemporary reality. After all, workers do receive regular advances on their personal income which are nothing other than a sort of fixed wage. In reality, every worker, when hired, individually negotiates his position on the grade scale and his chances for future advancement. In this bargaining process not only skills and conditions of work, but also labor market conditions are taken into consideration. Jobs difficult to fill tend to be classified higher on the grade scale, in order to attract workers with scarce skills to the firm. Thus market conditions are brought in through the back door. The need to justify the classification of new workers into specific grade scales forces management to

pressure the workers' council to approve *ex post* the promised "wage rate," which in some instances leads to corruption.

2. See B. Horvat, "Fundamentals of A Theory of Distribution in Self-Governing Socialism," *Economic Analysis and Workers' Management*, 1976, no. 1-2, p. 42.

3. This form of compromise, reached by the two groups via a democratic process of extensive debate and bargaining, is distinct from the "consensus" reached in a capitalist society where similar issues are settled via the labor market and the competition it implies.

4. See V. H. Vroom, "The Nature of the Relationship between Motivation and Performance," in V. H. Vroom and E. L. Deci, eds., *Management and Motivation* (New York: Penguin, 1977); idem, "Industrial Social Psychology," in ibid., pp. 392-415; H. Leibenstein, "Allocative Efficiency vs. X-Efficiency," *American Economic Review*, no. 56 (June 1966).

5. For more details see J. Vanek, *The General Theory of Labor-Managed Economies* (Ithaca: Cornell University Press, 1970) and J. C. Espinosa and A. S. Zimbalist, *Economic Democracy: Workers' Participation in Chilean Industry 1970-1973* (New York: Academic, 1978).

6. See O. E. Williamson, *Market and Hierarchies* (New York: The Free Press, 1975).

7. M. R. Carter, "Revisionist Lessons from the Peruvian Experience with Cooperative Agricultural Production," in D. C. Jones and Jan Svejnar, eds., *Advances in the Economic Analysis of Participatory and Labor Managed Firms*, vol. 1 (London: JAI Press, 1985), pp. 179-95.

8. See J. Obradović, "Distribution of Participation in the Process of Decision Making on Problems Related to the Economic Activity of the Company," in *Participation and Self-Management: Report of the First International Sociological Conference on Participation and Self-Management*, vol. 2 (Zagreb, 1972), pp. 136-64.

9. For more details see ibid., Tables 18, 19, 20, 21.

10. J. Županov, "Employees' Participation and Social Power in Industry," in *Participation and Self-Management*, vol. 1, pp. 33-41. See also J. Županov and A. S. Tennenbaum, "The Distribution of Control in some Yugoslav Industrial Organization," in A. S. Tennenbaum, ed., *Control and Organization* (New York: McGraw-Hill, 1966).

11. Županov, "Employees' Participation and Social Power in Industry," p. 40.

12. This point of view is expressed by R. Supek in "Two Types of Self-Managing Organization and Technological Progress," in *Participation and Self-Management*, vol. 1, pp. 150-74. A similar view is expressed by B. Fleas in "Yugoslavian Experience of Workers' Self-Management," in *Participation and Self-Management*, vol. 6 (1973).

13. Williamson, *Market and Hierarchies*, p. 46.

14. For more details see B. Horvat, "Two Widespread Ideological Deviations in Contemporary Yugoslav Society," *Eastern European Economics*, vol. 23, no. 1 (Fall 1984).

15. J. Županov, "Egalitarizam i industrijalizam" [Egalitarianism and Industrialism], in *Naše Teme*, no. 2 (1970); S. Bolčić, "The Value System of Participatory Economy," in *Participation and Self-Management*, vol. 2, pp. 97-122; I. Bićanić, "Nejednakosti i ličini dohoci" [Inequalities and Personal Income], in *Ekonomska politika*, no. 1718 (1985), pp. 24-26.

16. During my visit to Yugoslavia I was informed that some sort of guidelines were introduced, relating different categories of skill to unskilled labor, but were later abolished.

17. The share of personal income after taxation as a ratio of the total income of the enterprises declined from 46% in 1976 to 30% in 1982. In five years of crisis, 1979-1984, the state drastically reduced the share of net personal income in the total earned income of the enterprises. As a result much less was left to distribute among the employees. See M. Jovičić and B. Cerović, "Raspodela ličnih dohodaka i proizvodni rad" [The Distribution of Personal Income and Productive Labor], in *Raspodela prema radu protivrečnosti i perspektive* [Distribution According to Work: Contradictions and Perspectives] (Belgrade, 1983).

18. According to official statistics real personal income declined by nearly 35% in 1979-84.

19. Bićanić, "Nejednakosti i ličini dohoci."

IV. Interbranch Pay Differentials and Self-Management

1. This distinction between the labor and capital schools was first made by S. Estrin and W. Barlett in "The Effects of Enterprise Self-Management in Yugoslavia: An Empirical Survey," in D. C. Jones and J. Svejnar, eds., *Participatory and Self-Managed Firms: Evaluating Economic Performance* (Lexington: Lexington Books, 1982).

2. This stream of thought is represented by Benjamin Ward ("The Firm in Illyria-Market Socialism," *American Economic Review*, 1958, no. 4), J. E. Mead ("The Theory of Labour-Managed Firms and of Profit Sharing," *Economic Journal* no. 81, 1972), H. Wachtel ("Workers' Management and Inter-Industry Wage Differentials in Yugoslavia," *Journal of Political Economy*, vol. 3, no. 80 (1972), pp. 540-60), and particularly by S. Estrin (*Self-Management: Economic Theory and Yugoslav Practice* [Cambridge: Cambridge University Press, 1983]). A good presentation of the labor school view can be found in an article by Estrin and Jan Svejnar, "Explanations of Earnings in Yugoslavia: The Capital and Labor Schools Compared," *Economic Analysis and Workers' Management*, vol. 19, no. 1 (1985), pp. 1-12.

3. All three schools take for granted that there is a uniform maximand for all Yugoslav firms, an approach that can be seriously questioned on the following grounds:

First, the shortcoming of any uniform maximand as an accurate description of a firm's behavior. For more details see B. Btaszczyk and M. Dabrowski, "Efektywność ekonomiczna i spoteczna przedsisbiorstwa samorzadowego—mity i reczywistość" [The Economic and Social Effectiveness of the Self-managed Enterprise—Myth and Reality], *Ekonomista* 1985, no. 3; Jan Lipiński, *Funkcjonowanie rynku w nowym systemie gospodarowania* [The Functioning of the Market in the New Economic System] (Warsaw: P.T.E., 1982), pp. 7-9.

Second, the erroneous concept that what is true for the firm must also be true for the national economy as a whole. This objection to any uniform maximand is based on the fact that the existence of an aggregate maximand assumes a socioeconomic homogeneity of the collective which does not exist in the Yugoslav firm. The aims and objectives of different groups in the firm are not identical. We can, with some approximation, distinguish two groups with different objectives in the Yugoslav enterprise: (1) the stable group of employees interested in the long-term maximization of net income per worker, and (2) the fluid or unstable group of employees whose major aim is to maximize the short-term level of wages (personal income). The balance of forces between these two groups decides the real behavior of the firm. Compromises and fluctuations between their objectives are to be expected. This strict and rigid classification of groups with different objectives is, in many respects, a simplification of reality, but at least it underlines the fact of how difficult it is to establish an aggregate uniform behavioral principle of the firm.

Even if we assume that a single enterprise has a propensity to use capital-intensive and labor-saving techniques, as Ward suggests, due to the nature of its maximand, it does not automatically follow that on a macro scale (for all enterprises in the aggregate) there will be a smaller increase in employment than there would be in a capitalist economy. To assume so automatically means to commit the so-called error of aggregation—that the whole is always nothing more than a sum of its components. In many cases in economic life this is not so. What is true for the individual enterprise is not necessarily true for the socialized sector as a whole, because interaction among enterprises can create a new situation. It cannot be excluded that savings on labor in a single enterprise may be compensated by an increase in employment in another enterprise, due to an increase in demand for capital which is induced by capital-intensive techniques. In other words, labor replaced by machines may be hired to produce those machines.

4. See B. Horvat, "On the Theory of the Labor-Managed Firm," in B. Horvat, M. Marković, and R. Supek, eds., *Self-Governing Socialism: A Reader* (White Plains, NY: IASP [M. E. Sharpe], 1975) vol. 2, pp. 229-40; idem, *The Political Economy of Socialism: A Marxist Social Theory* (Armonk: M. E. Sharpe, 1982), p. 344; idem, "Farewell to the Illyrian Firm," *Economic Analysis and Workers' Management*, 1986, no. 1, pp. 23-29; idem, "The Theory of the Worker-Managed Firm Revisited," *Journal of Comparative Economics*, 1986, no. 10, pp. 9-25; idem, "The Illyrian Firm: An Alternative View—A Rejoinder," *Economic Analysis and Workers' Management*, vol. 20, no. 4 (1986), pp. 411-16; J. Vanek, *The General Theory of Labor-Managed Economies* (Ithaca: Cornell University Press, 1970); D. Dubravčić, *Ponasanje samoupravnog poduzece kod izbora kombinacije proizvodnich faktora* [The Behavior of the Self-managed Firm in Choosing the Combination of Factors of Production] (Zagreb, 1967); V. Tričković, "Naučno rukovodjene u samoupravljaniu—uslov efikasnog privredjivanja" [Scientific Management in a Self-governed Firm—As a Precondition of an Efficient Production Process], *Ekonomska misao*, 1969, no. 1.

In the Western literature, S. Rosefielde and W. Pfouts have also taken issue with the neoclassical Illyrian concept (see "The Firm in Illyria: Market Syndicalism Reconsidered," *Journal of Comparative Economics*, 1986, no. 10, pp. 160-70); as have Joan Robinson and H. Lydall (see "The Soviet Collective Farm as a Producer: Comment," *American Economic Review*, 1967, no. 57, pp. 222-23, and H. Lydall, *Yugoslav Socialism: Theory and Practice* [Oxford: Clarendon Press, 1984]).

5. In the three last articles published by Horvat in 1986 (as cited in the preceding note), the gist of his argument against the neoclassical static equibilibrium concept boils down to the following few points: (1) From the fact that income per worker (y) in the labor-managed firm is larger than wages (w) in its "twin" capitalist firm, Ward and his followers concluded that employment and output will be smaller in the self-managed firm than in its capitalist counterpart. This would be so, Horvat

argued, if all profit were distributed as wages. But this is not the case. The firm's behavior is connected not with the total income per worker but only with the distributed income, and this can be smaller, larger, or equal to that in its capitalist counterpart. (2) Those who see a strong correlation between the nature of the maximand and underemployment argue that enterprises under self-management tend to employ new workers only when newcomers will increase the average level of net labor productivity, something that is possible only when the new workers will produce more on the average than the already employed workers. Thus there is no material interest in taking on extra workers if the result would be a decline in average labor productivity of the firm. The reluctance to hire new workers as explained by the marginal theory is, however, static and timeless. But technological progress goes on all the time. New workers are employed in new technologies with higher labor productivities. Therefore, static comparison of marginal productivities of old and new workers are irrelevant. (3) The perception of the Yugoslav firm as a predominantly labor-saving one does not conform with reality. It is a well known fact that over-manning is widespread in Yugoslavia, because in a collectively managed enterprise, workers are reluctant to dismiss redundant workers—particularly themselves. As practice has shown, argues Horvat, in time of demand contraction or changing prices, firms would rather reduce wages and increase inventories than dismiss workers. Even when there is a reluctance to hire new employees it always goes hand in hand with the inability of management to fire workers. Workers' solidarity in the defense of their job security in the enterprise is well supported by the local authorities.

6. See J. Vanek, "The Yugoslav Economy Viewed through the Theory of Labor-Management," *World Development*, vol. 1, no. 9 (1973), pp. 39-56; J. Vanek and M. Jovičić, "The Capital Market and Income Distribution in Yugoslavia," *Quarterly Journal of Economics*, no. 89 (1975), pp. 432-43; D. D. Milenkovitch, *Plan and Market in Yugoslav Economic Thought* (New Haven: Yale University Press, 1971); R. Staellerts, "The Effects of Capital Intensity on Income in Yugoslav Industry," *Economic Analysis and Workers' Management*, no. 15 (1981), pp. 501-16.

7. This point is very strongly emphasized by S. Popov in "Intersectoral Relations of Personal Incomes," *Yugoslav Survey*, vol. 8, May 1972, pp. 63-80. She tries to prove that there is a very strong correlation between firms with high K/L ratios (usually large by any indicator of concentration) and their size of personal income.

8. See Vanek, "The Yugoslav Economy Viewed through the Theory of Labor-Management."

9. Other factors are the underdeveloped capital market, arbitrary limits on interest rates, and some of the social agreements.

10. Self-financing and low prices for capital in Yugoslavia are, according to Vanek in *The General Theory of Labor-Managed Economies* (Ithaca: Cornell University Press, 1970), also conducive to unemployment. Vanek rejects the claim of the labor school in general, and Ward in particular, that the maximand of the Yugoslav firm is the cause of unemployment. The villain is not the objective function of the firm, but the wrong prices for capital and the wrong way capital is financed, which affects employment negatively via the increase of the capital-labor ratio. If the working collective is paying very little or nothing for capital, it will try to maximize productivity per worker without changing the size of the labor force. By

doing so, each member will maximize income. But if the firm must pay a reasonable price for the same capital, it will be in everybody's interest to exploit the capital more intensely by increasing employment, because as long as the new members' productivity is still positive it makes it easier for the old members to pay the cost of rented capital.

To alleviate the unemployment problem the economy must create new firms; new capital must be available for those who are seeking employment. But self-financing is an obstacle to capital availability for those who have no work. If loanable funds and internal accumulation are all in the hands of the existing firms, the unemployed may never have access to funds. Moreover, existing firms may be reluctant to create new autonomous labor-managed firms, because they would have to part with their own funds and then lose control over them.

By contrast, if all loanable funds are externally supplied at scarcity prices, those seeking jobs will have an advantage in competing for those funds because they live on low incomes and the loan conditions may be acceptable to them. In other words, creation of new autonomous firms is strengthened by external financing. Even old firms will be more inclined than before to create new independent firms. Experience has shown, according to Vanek, that when control over capital rests with the existing producers, either directly in the form of their own investment funds or indirectly through their influence on the policies of banks in which they are depositors, very few firms—and along with this very few jobs—are created.

External funding has another advantage, in that requests for capital would be examined by external experts who would ensure that the projects were economically sound and properly designed.

11. For more details see B. Gui, "Limits of External Financing: A Model and Application to Labor-Managed Firms," in D. C. Jones and J. Svejnar, eds., *Advances in the Economic Analysis of Participatory and Labor-Managed Firms*, vol. 1 (Connecticut: JAI Press, 1985).

12. See J. P. Bonin, "Labour Management and Capital Maintenance: Investment Decision in the Socialist Labour Managed Firm," in ibid.

13. See M. Kamušić, "Economic Efficiency and Workers' Self-Management," in M. J. Brockmeyer, ed. *Yugoslav Workers' Self-Management* (Dordrecht: Reidel, 1970).

14. The fact that more than half of all investments are now funded by credit creates a high debt-service burden, which in turn leads to further borrowing. Credit payments very often equal or surpass the current net accumulation of the enterprises; hence investment from the firm's own funds is sufficient only to cover depreciation capital. Needless to say, constant pressure on the banks for more credit is inflationary. This process is aggravated by liquidity problems, due to the fact that many enterprises repay their debt behind schedule or not at all. For more details see National Account, *Yugoslav Survey*, no. 3, August 1984, pp. 43-56.

15. Although the marginal capital-output ratio has increased in other socialist countries (especially the USSR and Poland) more dramatically than in Yugoslavia, the deterioration of investment efficiency measured by the marginal capital output ratio (the ratio of the gross investment in fixed assets and stocks to the increase in gross domestic product) was far from negligible in Yugoslavia. In the period 1957-1977 this magnitude grew, for the total Yugoslav economy, from 2.7 in 1953-61 to 3.9 in 1962-77. What is more important, the marginal capital-output ratio varies substantially in the different republics. This magnitude is, by and large,

inversely related to the stage of development. The more developed republics and provinces have lower capital-output ratios. Kosovo, Montenegro, Macedonia, and Bosnia all have capital-output ratios above the national average. See D. Vojnić, "Investment Policy," in Radmila Stojanović, ed., *The Functioning of the Yugoslav Economy* (Armonk: M. E. Sharpe, 1982). The efficiency of investment deteriorated even further after 1977 and in 1980-83 this deterioration accelerated. See "Economic Development 1971-1983," *Yugoslav Survey*, May 1984, pp. 61-79.

16. See A. Bajt, "Društvena svojina—kolektivna i individualna" [Social Ownership—Collective and Individual], *Gledišta*, vol. 9, no. 4 (1968), pp. 531-44; B. Horvat, *Towards a Theory of a Planned Economy* (White Plains: IASP [M. E. Sharpe], 1964); K. Mihailović, *Ekonomska stvarnost Jugoslavije* [The Economic Reality of Yugoslavia] (Belgrade, 1982); Popov, "Intersectoral Relations of Personal Income."

17. Yugoslavs do not call their socialized enterprise a cooperative, but an "organization of associated labor." The intent here is to distinguish the Yugoslav firm from the cooperative form as far as property rights are concerned. Members of the Yugoslav enterprise do not have individual control over their invested capital as is the case in a cooperative.

18. It is difficult not to agree with Peter Wiles when he claims that the typical supporter of reinvesting will be the skilled and influential middle-aged worker with a family and a satisfactory house and possibly active membership on the workers' council. The typical voter for more personal income will be the uninfluential, the mobile workers, etc.

19. For more details see H. Lydall, *Yugoslav Socialism*, pp. 215-18.

20. See E. G. Furubotn and S. Pejović, "Property Rights and the Behavior of the Firm in a Socialist State: The Example of Yugoslavia," *Zeitschrift für National-Ekonomie*, no. 30 (1970), pp. 431-54; "Property Rights, Economic Decentralization, and the Evolution of the Yugoslav Firm, 1965-1972," *Journal of Law and Economics*, October 1973, no. 16; S. Pejović, "The Firm, Monetary Policy and Property Rights in a Planned Economy," *Western Economic Journal*, September 1969, pp. 193-200.

21. It is assumed that a third alternative does not exist—namely the alternative to invest in the private sector. This is very peculiar in a country where 40% of the workers have their own agricultural holdings.

22. This terminology, first used to describe the property relations in the firm by J. Vanek ("Identifying the Participatory Economy," in *Self-Governing Socialism*, vol. 2), tries to distinguish between ownership of capital assets and the right to enjoy the fruits of material goods which are their ownership in the traditional sense of the word. In this context it is worthwhile to mention A. Bajt's concept of the nature of capital in the Yugoslav system. Bajt distinguished ownership of capital from ownership of the particular physical means of production. Society is the owner of capital but the owner of the physical means of production is the collective of the firm. See Bajt, "Social Ownership—Collective and Individual," in *Self-Governing Socialism*, vol. 2, pp. 151-63.

23. Vanek, who disregards the stagnation concept of the property rights school, claims that the time horizon of an average Yugoslav firm is very long. See Vanek, *General Theory of Labor-Managed Economies*.

24. Furubotn and Pejović have calculated that to make investment in nonowned capital as attractive to the workers as savings deposits at 5%, the return from

investment in nonowned capital must be 23%, 19%, 13%, and 9% respectively for the time horizons 5, 6, 10, and 15 years.

25. For more detail see T. Eger and P. Weisse, "Einzel- und gesamtwirt-schaftliche Aspekte des Investitionsverhaltens Arbeiterselbstverwaltungsunternehmen," in J. Backhaus, T. Eger, and H. G. Nutzinger, *Partizipation in Betrieb und Gesellschaft* (Frankfurt/New York: Campus Verlag, 1978). Eger and Weisse also propose measures to overcome the lack of propensity to accumulate by the collective of the enterprise. They suggest participation in the income from investment for a particular period even if the worker leaves the firm. They believe that this would broaden the time horizon of the workers in making accumulation decisions, which would reduce the attractiveness of choosing to invest in personal deposits rather than in nonowned assets. But such payment would necessitate settling the value of the shares and a method for transferring them to the next generation of employees.

26. See J. Strzelecki, "Teoria praw własnosci: geneza, podstawowe pojecia i twierdzenia, uwagi o zastosowaniu do analizy gospodarki socialistycznej" [The Property Rights Theory: Genesis, Basic Concept, and Postulates. Remarks about Applicability to Analysis of the Socialist Economy], a paper delivered at the conference *Systemy wlasność a proces gospodarowania* [Property Systems and the Economic Process], published by IRG, SGPIS (Warsaw, 1984); J. Staniszkis, "Prawo własnośći w socializmie i ich ekonomiczne, społeczne i polityczne implikacje" [Property Rights in Socialism: Their Economic, Social, and Political Implications] (paper delivered at a conference in Warsaw, February 1985). This approach is logically consistent if we are assuming that enterprises are acting under soft budget constraints, which in this context means the possibility of not repaying the loan. It is difficult to prejudge how the firm would behave if conditions of repayment were strictly enforced. Would the self-managed firm still have a high propensity to borrow and invest?

27. Due to the crisis, many enterprises do not even have enough net income to pay fixed wages, to say nothing of saving.

28. Total investment in fixed capital financed by bank credit has increased from 32% in 1964 to 39% in 1966, 47% in 1968, and 51% in 1971. See Branko Horvat, *The Yugoslav Economic System* (White Plains: IASP [M. E. Sharpe], 1976), p. 222, Table 28. At the same time, we observe a sharp increase in personal savings from 10% to 36% of the gross national savings. See D. Dimitrijević, "Mechanizam finansiranje Jugoslavenske privrede" [The Mechanism of Financing the Yugoslav Economy], *Ekonomska misao*, 1973, pp. 25-45.

29. See Horvat, "The Illyrian Firm: An Alternative View," p. 145. L. Madžar (in the same issue of *Economic Analysis and Workers' Management*) questioned Horvat's point of view, claiming that the low propensity to save is bound with the specific property rights of the self-managed firm as described by Furubotn and Pejović. This view is shared by M. Milovanović; see *Kapital i minuli rad* [Capital and Past Labor] (Belgrade: Savremena administracija, 1986).

30. See an interesting discussion by F. H. Stephen, "Property Rights and the Labor-Managed Firm in the Long Run," *Economic Analysis and Workers' Management*, vol. 13, 1979, pp. 149-66.

31. O. Šik, "Marktwirtschaft ohne kapitalismus," in W. Fricke and A. Geissler, eds., *Demokratisierung der Wirtschaft* (Marburg, 1973). A. Nove moves in a similar direction in his book *The Economics of Feasible Socialism* (London: George Allen and Unwin, 1983), pp. 216-17. Nove proposed a weaker variant of the system used

in the Mondragon cooperatives in Spain, namely a length-of-service bonus linked with the long-term level of profit or the value of basic assets, paid to the worker when he leaves the enterprise. The length-of-service bonus is a form of recovering one's accumulated capital. In the Mondragon network of cooperatives, those who join make a sizable contribution of initial capital, which earns a rate of interest repayable when the member leaves the cooperative. Furthermore, all initial capital contributions by members of the cooperative are of equal magnitude. This guarantees that the amount returned after leaving the enterprise will vary only with the length of service. Major contribution to the capital assets by the members makes them materially interested in the long-term perspective of the firm, and also gives them an interest in the investment process. For more details see H. Thomas and C. Logan, *Mondragon* (London: Allen and Unwin, 1982).

32. The major proponent of this view in Hungary is M. Tardos. See "Property Rights in Hungary," a paper delivered at the international conference "Plan and/or Market," organized by the Institut für die Wissenschaften vom Menschen in Vienna, November 13-20, 1988.

33. These ideas are expressed by Gui ("Limits of External Financing"); L. Putterman ("On Some Recent Explanations of Why Capital Hires Labor," *Inquiry*, no. 22 (1984), pp. 171-87); F. H. Stephen ("Property Rights and the Labor-Managed Firm in the Long Run"), and others.

34. See the eleven proposals drawn from federal documents as listed in chapter I of the present study.

V. Conclusions: Is Self-Management the Villain?

1. Command economies also have substantial interbranch differentials, but they are established by the center in accordance with its preferences. What is more, the differentials are in most cases and most of the time smaller than in market-oriented systems.

2. For more detail see A. Kruger and S. Summers, "Efficiency Wages and the Inter-Industry Wage Structure" (mimeo, Harvard 1986). See also idem, "Reflection on the Inter-Industry Wage Structure," in K. Lang and J. S. Leonard, eds. *Unemployment and the Structure of Labour Markets* (Cambridge: Basil Blackwell, 1987); W. T. Dickens and L. F. Katz, "Inter-Industry Wage Differences and Industry Characteristics," in ibid., and K. M. Murphy and R. H. Topel, "Unemployment, Risk, and Earnings: Testing for Equalizing Wage Differences in the Labor Market," in ibid.

3. U.S. Department of Labor, Bureau of Labor Statistics, 1985.

4. A full survey of efficiency wage theories can be found in L. F. Katz, "Efficiency Wage Theories: A Partial Evaluation," in S. Fischer, ed., *National Bureau of Economic Research Macroeconomics Annual 1986* (Cambridge: MIT Press).

5. Kalecki can be considered a pioneer of the efficiency wage concept. In his seminal paper of 1943, "Political Aspects of Full Employment" (in *Selected Essays in the Dynamics of the Capitalist Economy, 1933–1970* [Cambridge: Cambridge University Press, 1971]), Kalecki claims that unemployment is necessary to maintain work discipline and work intensity on the shop floor.

6. On the fair wage concept see G. A. Akerlof and J. L. Yellen, "Fairness and Unemployment," *American Economic Review*, Papers and Proceedings, May 1988, pp. 44-49.

7. See S. Estrin, *Self-Management: Economic Theory and Yugoslav Practice* (Cambridge: Cambridge University Press, 1983), Appendix B, Table B4.

International comparisons made by Kruger and Summers (''Efficiency Wages and the Inter-Industry Wage Structure,'' Tables 2.3 and 2.4), using different econometric tools from Estrin's, indicate that in many Western countries the dispersion of wages among branches is larger than in Yugoslavia.

8. Some well-known Yugoslav economists, including Horvat, Bajt, and B. Marendić, believe that it would be possible to guarantee enterprises equal economic opportunity only if worker collectives were permitted to retain only those net incomes which are a result of their labor contribution and quality of management, and not effects linked with better capital endowment and market conditions. It should be stressed, however, that the concepts of labor contribution used here are ambiguous. In one instance the labor contribution means effort, intensity of work, education, and skill; in another it means the result of work in terms of output. See A. Bajt, ''Dohodna cena kak normalna cena u našoj privredi'' [Income Price as a Normal Price in Our Economy], *Ekonomist*, 1964, no. 4; B. Horvat, ''Raspodjela prema radu medu kolektivima'' [The Distribution According to Work between Collectives], *Naša stvarnosta*, no. 1 (1962), pp. 52-66; idem, ''Fundamentals of a Theory of Distribution in Self-Governing Socialism,'' *Economic Analysis and Workers' Management*, 1976, nos. 1-2.

The dominant group of economists in Yugoslavia believes that net income of the enterprise should contain at least a part or all effects from monopoly power on the market and other forms of monopoly. See for example M. Korać, *Problemi teorije i prakse socijalisticke robne proizvodnje u Jugoslaviji* [Problems of Theory and Practice of Socialist Material Production in Yugoslovia] (Zagreb, 1965).

9. See J. Wecławski, *System cen w Jugoslawii* [The Price System in Yugoslavia] (Lublin: UMCS, 1984), p. 27, Table 4.